UNDERSTANDING

God's Promises

LARRY RICHARDS
AND
C. H. SPURGEON
(Updated by Roy H. Clarke)

THOMAS NELSON PUBLISHERS
Nashville

Understanding God's Promises © 2004 by Thomas Nelson, Inc.

Selections in this volume are taken from *Every Promise in the Bible,* © 1998 by Lawrence O. Richards, and *Beside Still Waters,* © 1999 by Thomas Nelson, Inc., and have been organized and edited by George W. Knight.

Published in Nashville, Tennessee, by Thomas Nelson, Inc.

Interior design by Bob Bubnis/BookSetters

Richards, Larry, 1931-
Spurgeon, C. H. (Charles Haddon), 1834–1892
    Understanding God's promises / Larry Richards and C. H. Spurgeon (updated by Roy H. Clarke)

ISBN 0-7852-5099-9

Printed in Canada

1 2 3 4 5 6 7—08 07 06 05 04

TABLE OF CONTENTS

INTRODUCTION 8

GOD'S PROMISES TO BLESS ME

GOD SHOWERS ME WITH HIS "GOOD GIFTS" 10
GOD LOVES ME IN SPITE OF MY SIN 12
GOD GIVES ME WISDOM AND UNDERSTANDING 14
GOD FILLS MY LIFE WITH JOY AND MEANING 16
GOD CALMS MY ANXIETIES 18
GOD SUSTAINS ME BY HIS COMPASSION 20
GOD GRANTS ME REST WHEN I FOLLOW HIS LEADING 22
GOD GIVES ME AN EASY YOKE TO CARRY 24
GOD GIVES ME PEACE THAT SURPASSES UNDERSTANDING 26
GOD MAKES ME CONTENT WITH WHAT I HAVE 28
GOD PROVIDES A UNIVERSAL GOSPEL THAT INCLUDES ME 30
GOD GRANTS ME ACCESS TO HIM THROUGH THE HOLY SPIRIT 32
GOD PROVIDES A MEDIATOR WHO CARES FOR ME 34
JESUS PROVIDES ME A HELPER LIKE HIMSELF 36
GOD FILLS MY LIFE WITH THE FRUIT OF THE SPIRIT 38
GOD HEARS AND ANSWERS MY PRAYERS 40
GOD NOURISHES ME SPIRITUALLY 42
JESUS CARES ABOUT MY MATERIAL NEEDS 44
GOD GRANTS ME ETERNAL LIFE 46

GOD'S PROMISES TO PROTECT ME

GOD GUARDS AND KEEPS ME 48
GOD IS MY SHIELD AND REWARD 50
GOD GIVES ME MERCY AND GRACE IN TIMES OF NEED 52
GOD WALKS WITH ME THROUGH THE FIRE 54
GOD SHELTERS ME FROM HIS WRATH 56
GOD CARES FOR MY LOVED ONES 58
GOD PROTECTS ME FROM THE EVIL ONE 60
GOD CALMS MY FEARS 62
GOD WILL WATCH OVER ME WHEN I AM OLD 64
GOD TAKES AWAY MY FEAR OF DEATH 66
GOD WILL TAKE ME TO BE WITH HIM AFTER I DIE 68

UNDERSTANDING GOD'S PROMISES

GOD'S PROMISES TO DELIVER ME

GOD HEARS ME IN MY TIME OF TROUBLE 70
GOD DELIVERS ME FROM SELF-PITY 72
GOD DELIVERS ME FROM SATAN'S POWER 74
GOD GIVES ME VICTORY OVER TEMPTATION 76
GOD GRANTS ME FREEDOM THROUGH HIS TRUTH 78
GOD TRANSFORMS MY LIFE THROUGH HIS SPIRIT 80
GOD MINISTERS TO ME THROUGH DIVINE MESSENGERS 82
GOD RAISES UP OTHERS TO SHARE MY BURDENS 84
GOD GRANTS ME INNER PEACE 86
GOD GOES INTO BATTLE ON MY BEHALF 88

GOD'S PROMISES TO GUIDE ME

GOD GUIDES ME LIKE A SHEPHERD 90
GOD GIVES ME ACCESS TO THE MIND OF CHRIST 92
GOD FILLS ME WITH HIS WISDOM 94
GOD HELPS ME MAKE TOUGH DECISIONS .96
GOD WORKS WITH ME TO RESOLVE CONFLICTS 98
GOD HELPS ME TO DISCERN HIS WILL 100
GOD INFLUENCES ME THROUGH GODLY ROLE MODELS 102
GOD GUIDES ME INTO HIS REST 104
GOD INSTRUCTS ME THROUGH HIS SPIRIT 106
GOD GUIDES ME INTO ALL TRUTH 108

GOD'S PROMISES TO STRENGTHEN ME

GOD GIVES ME HOPE IN A HOPELESS SITUATION 110
GOD STRENGTHENS ME TO DO HIS WORK 112
GOD ENABLES ME TO RESIST TEMPTATION 114
GOD GIVES ME HIS FAVOR 116
GOD GIVES ME PATIENCE UNDER PERSECUTION 118
GOD IS MY HELPER WHO NEVER FAILS 120
GOD REFINES ME IN THE FURNACE OF AFFLICTION 122
GOD HELPS ME COPE WITH PAIN AND SORROW 124
GOD STRENGTHENS MY FAITH THROUGH AFFLICTION 126
GOD MAKES ME STRONGER THROUGH DIVINE DISCIPLINE 128

TABLE OF CONTENTS

GOD'S PROMISES TO HEAL ME

GOD OFFERS ME FORGIVENESS AND HEALING THROUGH HIS GRACE . . .130
GOD HEALS MY TENDENCY TO WANDER AWAY FROM HIM 132
GOD LIFTS ME UP IN TIMES OF DEPRESSION 134
GOD HEALS MY BROKEN HEART 136
GOD RESTORES MY FALTERING FAITH 138
THE GOD OF PEACE FILLS MY LIFE WITH PEACE 140
GOD RESTORES MY LOSSES 142
GOD GRANTS HEALING THROUGH THE POWER OF PRAYER 144
GOD REPLACES MY WEAKNESS WITH HIS STRENGTH 146

GOD'S PROMISES TO HONOR ME AS A
PERSON OF WORTH

GOD CREATED ME FOR FELLOWSHIP WITH HIM THROUGH CHRIST . .148
GOD LOVES ME WITH AN EVERLASTING LOVE 150
GOD INCLUDES ME IN HIS SALVATION PLAN 152
GOD CREATED ME TO HAVE A PERSONAL RELATIONSHIP WITH HIM . .154
GOD KEEPS ME IN FELLOWSHIP WITH HIM THROUGH CHRIST 156
GOD GIVES ME HIS PERSONAL ATTENTION 158
GOD ACCEPTS ME AS ONE OF HIS CHILDREN 160
GOD WORKS FOR MY GOOD 162

GOD'S PROMISES TO REDEEM ME

GOD CLEANSES ME FROM SIN 164
GOD SAVES ME FROM HIS WRATH 166
GOD PROVIDES ACCESS TO SALVATION THROUGH HIS SON 168
GOD FORGIVES ME 170
GOD PROVIDES ATONEMENT FOR MY SINS 172
GOD SAVES ME THROUGH A SACRIFICIAL DEATH 174
GOD DECLARES ME RIGHTEOUS ON THE BASIS OF PERSONAL FAITH . .176
GOD DECLARES ME BLAMELESS BEFORE CHRIST 178
GOD MAKES ME A NEW CREATION 180
GOD REFRESHES ME WITH LIVING WATER 182
GOD FEEDS ME WITH THE BREAD OF LIFE 184
GOD RESTORES ME TO HIS FELLOWSHIP 186
GOD GIVES ME A NEW SELF 188
GOD CONTINUES TO TRANSFORM MY LIFE 190

GOD'S PROMISES TO COMFORT AND ASSURE ME

GOD IS FAITHFUL IN SPITE OF MY UNFAITHFULNESS 192
GOD TAKES AWAY MY WORRY 194
GOD CONSOLES ME IN MY GRIEF 196
GOD GIVES ME VICTORY OVER PAIN AND DEATH 198
GOD ANSWERS MY PRAYERS WHEN THEY REFLECT HIS WILL 200
GOD CARES FOR ME LIKE A TENDER SHEPHERD 202
GOD ASSURES ME THAT I WILL NEVER BE SEPARATED FROM HIS LOVE . .204
GOD WILL KEEP ME SAFE IN THE SAVIOR'S HANDS 206
GOD WILL NOT FORSAKE ME 208
GOD GIVES ME HOPE FOR THE FUTURE 210
GOD PROMISES ME A BETTER LIFE BEYOND THE GRAVE 212
GOD ASSURES ME THAT JESUS WILL COME AGAIN 214
GOD WILL REUNITE ME WITH MY LOVED ONES 216

GOD'S PROMISES TO USE ME IN HIS SERVICE

GOD GIVES ME IMPORTANT WORK TO DO IN HIS KINGDOM 218
GOD BLESSES ME WITH GIFTS TO BE USED FOR HIM 220
GOD WILL GIVE ME THE STRENGTH TO DO HIS WORK 222
GOD ASSURES MY SUCCESS IN DOING KINGDOM WORK 224
GOD MAKES ME PRODUCTIVE IN HIS SERVICE 226
GOD USES MY WEAKNESS FOR HIS GLORY .228
GOD BLESSES OTHERS THROUGH MY TRIALS 230
GOD GUARANTEES MY CONTINUING USEFULNESS IN HIS SERVICE . . .232
GOD WILL REWARD ME FOR WORK DONE FOR HIM 234

GOD'S PROMISES TO BE WITH ME

GOD IS ALWAYS WITH ME 236
GOD IS THERE WHEN THINGS GO WRONG .238
GOD IS INVOLVED IN MY DAILY STRUGGLES 240
GOD SURROUNDS ME WITH HIS LOVE 242
GOD WILL NOT FORGET ME 244
JESUS GUIDES ME WITH HIS LIGHT 246
GOD DRAWS ME CLOSE TO HIMSELF 248
GOD IS WATCHING OVER ME 250

TABLE OF CONTENTS

GOD'S PROMISES TO REWARD ME

God Will Give Me a Place in Heaven Prepared by Jesus 252

God Will Give Me a Guaranteed Inheritance 254

God Will Give Me Heavenly Treasures Rather
    Than Earthly Riches 256

God Accepts Me as One of His Children 258

God Will Show Me the Full Revelation of
    Jesus in the Future 260

God Promises That I Will Appear with Jesus in Glory 262

God Will Reward My Labors of Love for Others 264

God Will Give Me Eternal Life 266

God Will Give Me a Crown of Righteousness 268

God Will Give Me a Glorious Spiritual Body 270

Topical Index 273

Scripture Index 282

INTRODUCTION

In his prayer of dedication for the newly constructed temple in Jerusalem, King Solomon declared:

> Blessed be the Lord, who has given rest to His people Israel, according to all that He promised. There has not failed one word of all His good promises, which He promised through His servant Moses (1 Kin. 8:56).

Like believers of all generations, Solomon had discovered a wonderful truth about the Lord: He is a promise-making God who always lives up to His promises. From the beginning of time into eternity, He has proven faithful to His people. Friends may desert us and even family members may let us down, but we can count on Him and His promises to sustain us in our times of need.

This book is a guide to the most important divine promises from the Bible. It goes beyond just quoting Scripture passages that contain God's promises. Here you will find a thorough explanation of each of these promises and what it means for your daily life. The index at the back of the book will help you find God's promises for specific life needs such as Affliction, Depression, Forgiveness, Loneliness, and Salvation.

Dwight L. Moody once said, "Let a man feed for a month on the promises of God, and he will not talk about how poor he is." *Understanding God's Promises* will make you realize how enriched and blessed you are through the eternal promises of the living Lord.

GOD SHOWERS ME WITH HIS "GOOD GIFTS"

*"And I say to you, ask, and it will be given to you;
seek, and you will find; knock, and it will be opened
to you."*

—LUKE 11:9

The broad context of this prayer promise is the Sermon
on the Mount, in which Jesus explained the righteousness, mercy, sincerity, humility, and love expected of a
kingdom citizen. The promise itself is more closely
defined by the illustration of the good human father,
and by Jesus' observation that God surely knows how
to give "good gifts" to those who ask Him (Matt. 7:11).

Note that in Luke's version of this teaching of
Jesus, Jesus' teaching concludes with the promise of
the Holy Spirit rather than the "good gifts" in
Matthew's report (see Luke 11:9–13). This is not a conflict. Christ must have preached this basic message
many times to different crowds during His three-year
public ministry. He probably varied His words and

expressions from time to time. At the same time, there is real harmony between the report of the two Gospel writers. After all, it is the Holy Spirit's empowering presence that enables the believer to receive the "good gifts" of righteousness, humility, love, etc. of which Matthew wrote.

The limits of this prayer promise are defined by both the larger context and the immediate context. Those who approach God seeking humility, love, etc., will surely be given these gifts by a loving heavenly Father.

God does not answer selfish or sinful prayers. James wrote, "You ask and do not receive, because you ask amiss, that you may spend it on your [sinful] pleasures" (James 4:3). Yet when we actively approach God seeking His *good* gifts, we can be sure that He hears and responds.

—*Larry Richards*

GOD LOVES ME IN SPITE OF MY SIN

"Because he [Ahab] has humbled himself before Me, I will not bring the calamity in his days."

—1 KINGS 21:29

King Ahab of Israel had been given proof of God's presence and power. Rather than repent, he continued to act wickedly. The prophet Elijah confronted Ahab in Naboth's vineyard and announced God's judgment. Ahab's descendants would die, and his blood would stain the vineyard which the king had obtained by murdering Naboth.

This time Ahab was terrified. He showed that he believed God's word by tearing his clothes, wearing sackcloth, fasting, and mourning (1 Kin. 21:27). This was the traditional way the people of Bible times showed remorse and sorrow. God then sent Elijah to Ahab again, noting "how Ahab has humbled himself before Me." By his actions Ahab showed that he believed God would punish as He had said. Even this dim glimmer of belief in God's Word was enough to move God to delay the punishment. The ordained calamity would come, but not in Ahab's lifetime.

The incident gives us an amazing insight into God's grace. Even the most wicked people who humble themselves before the Lord will be treated more kindly than their actions deserve. If God was so kind to King Ahab, whose entire life was dedicated to wickedness, He will certainly be gracious to us when we sin.

Those who let sins drive them away from God make a tragic mistake. God knows our failings, but He loves us anyway. Any believer who humbles himself and returns to the Lord will be welcomed and fully restored. As the apostle John wrote, "If we confess our sins, He is faithful and just to forgive our sins and to cleanse us from all unrighteousness" (1 John 1:9).

—*Larry Richards*

GOD GIVES ME WISDOM AND UNDERSTANDING

*"I have given you a wise and understanding heart . . .
and I have also given you what you have not asked:
both riches and honor, so that there shall not be anyone like you among the kings all your days."*

1 KINGS 3:12, 13

When Solomon took the throne, God invited him to make a request. Solomon asked for "an understanding heart to judge Your people, that I may discern between good and evil" (1 Kin. 3:9). This unselfish response pleased the Lord, who granted it and added the blessings of wealth and long life.

Solomon was not asking for intelligence. He was asking for wisdom to discern what would be beneficial for the nation he led ["good"] and what would be harmful ["evil"]. This distinction between intelligence and wisdom is made throughout the Bible. While Solomon was given great intelligence (cf. 1 Kin. 4:29–34), what he was promised by the Lord was *wisdom*.

While this promise was made specifically to King Solomon, there are parallel promises in the New Testament that should encourage us. James tells us that "if any of you lacks wisdom, let him ask God, who gives to all liberally and without reproach, and it will be given to him" (James 1:5). And Jesus encouraged us to set priorities similar to Solomon's when He said, "Seek first the kingdom of God and His righteousness, and all these things shall be added to you" (Matt. 6:33).

Solomon's story is especially encouraging. How richly God blesses those who make His priorities their own!

Seeing the promise God gave Solomon should fill us with expectation. How confidently we can make God's priorities our own! We cannot lose by putting God first. We can only gain.

—*Larry Richards*

GOD FILLS MY LIFE WITH JOY AND MEANING

"For if these things are yours and abound, you will be neither barren nor unfruitful in the knowledge of our Lord Jesus Christ."

2 PETER 1:8

Peter referred to the "exceeding great and precious promises" that believers have been given in the gospel. Specifically, Peter said, "His divine power has given to us all things that pertain to life and godliness." We have been granted in Christ all we need to live godly lives.

But these promises call us to make commitments of our own. We are to work diligently at adding to our basic faith in Christ such virtues as knowledge, self-control, perseverance, godliness, brotherly kindness, and love. These are the qualities that make a Christian's life fruitful.

The promise of fruitfulness is conditional. We are to work diligently at living the Christian life. At the same time, we must not assume that the call to diligence means we should live the Christian life on our own. Peter said that God's divine power has given us "all things that pertain to life and godliness." The diligent life is a life of faith, in which we draw on Christ's strength even as we commit ourselves to the disciplines of Christian living.

Christ told His followers, "Abide in Me, and I in you. As the branch cannot bear fruit of itself, unless it abides in the vine, neither can you, unless you abide in Me" (John 15:4).

If we make an unqualified commitment to Jesus, our lives will be fruitful and productive. Life will have fresh meaning for us as well as others.

—*Larry Richards*

GOD CALMS MY ANXIETIES

"In the multitude of my anxieties within me, Your comforts delight my soul."

PSALM 94:19

Some of you are perplexed with a multitude of anxieties about your life. You do not know what to do. One plan was suggested, and for a time it seemed the best action. But now you have doubts. You are bewildered and you cannot see providence's clue. You are lost in a maze. Indeed, at this moment, you are depressed.

You have tried various ways and methods to escape your present difficulty. But you have been disappointed and are distracted. Your thoughts have no order; they drag you in opposite directions. The currents meet and twist as if you were in a whirlpool.

My perplexed friend, remember the children of Israel at the Red Sea. The sea was before them, rocks were on either side, and the cruel Egyptians roared in the rear. Imitate Israel's actions. "Do not be afraid. Stand still, and see the salvation of the Lord, which He will accomplish for you today" (Ex. 14:13). You reply,

"I cannot be quiet. I am agitated, perturbed, perplexed, tossed, and distracted. What shall I do?"

"In the multitude of my anxieties within me, Your comforts delight my soul" (Ps. 94:19). Turn your eyes to the deep things of God. Cease from an anxious consideration of seen things, which are temporary, and gaze by faith on things that are eternal.

Remember, your way is ordered by a higher power than your will and choice. The eternal God has fixed your every step. All things are fixed by the Father's hand. He who loved us from before the foundation of the world has determined every step of our pilgrimage.

It is a blessed thing, after you have been muddling and meddling with your anxieties, to throw your burdens on the Lord and leave them there.

—*Charles Haddon Spurgeon*

GOD SUSTAINS ME BY HIS COMPASSION

"Though He causes grief, yet He will show compassion according to the multitude of His mercies."

LAMENTATIONS 3:32

Great sorrow can stun, and it can make you forget the best source of consolation. A little blow can cause great pain. Yet I have heard that in assaults serious blows do not cause pain because they have destroyed consciousness. Extreme distress can rob you of your wits and make you forget your source of relief. Under the chastening rod, the pain is remembered and the healing promise is forgotten.

When they were under God's affliction, the people of Israel failed to remember His covenant because of the crushing effect of their sorrow and despair. Is that how it is with you? Has your ear grown dull through grief? Has your heart forgotten because of heaviness? Does your affliction seem more real than God? Does the black sorrow that covers you eclipse all the light of heaven and earth?

May I be my Master's messenger? Let me remind you that He is still in covenant with you. "Though He causes grief, yet He will show compassion according to the multitude of His mercies" (Lam. 3:32). It is written, "We know that all things work together for good to those who love God, to those who are the called according to His purpose" (Rom. 8:28). He will keep His Word!

The Lord has also said, "When you pass through the waters, I will be with you; and through the rivers, they shall not overflow you. When you walk through the fire, you shall not be burned, nor shall the flame scorch you" (Is. 43:2).

Depend on it; He will sustain you. Brush those tears away, anoint your head, wash you face, and be of good courage (2 Sam. 12:20). The Lord will strengthen your heart.

—Charles Haddon Spurgeon

GOD GRANTS ME REST
WHEN I FOLLOW HIS
LEADING

*"Stand in the ways and see, and ask for the old paths,
where the good way is, and walk in it; then you will
find rest for your souls."*

JEREMIAH 6:16

Chapter 6 of Jeremiah contains one of the prophet's predictions of disaster. Because of Judah's sins, national destruction had become certain. The only hope for Judah was to return to the traditional values in God's Law, and to walk in these values. But Judah rejected this appeal and said, "We will not walk in it."

This promise was addressed to the nation, and it is conditional. If God was to bless the nation, there had to be a return to what we today might call "traditional" values. Here the "old paths, where the good way is" are the paths defined in God's Law. Loyalty to God and commitment to His values are essential to national health and well-being.

Two principles underlie this promise. The first is that under the Mosaic Covenant God was obligated to bless when a generation walked in the "old paths." The second is that because God's moral laws function in any society, any nation that strays far from God's values will experience serious social breakdown. In our society today, the call to return to the old paths, as rooted in our Judeo-Christian heritage, can be expressed with the same urgency.

The promise as given has a national focus. Society itself must turn back to the old ways if the nation is to survive. Yet there are implications for the individual as well. Any person seeking rest must choose God's ways as his or her own. And if we do not? Isaiah reminds us that "'the wicked are like the troubled sea, when it cannot rest. . . . There is no peace,' says my God, 'for the wicked'" (Is. 57:20, 21).

—*Larry Richards*

GOD GIVES ME AN EASY YOKE TO CARRY

"Come to Me, all you who labor and are heavy laden,
and I will give you rest."

MATTHEW 11:28

Jesus thanked God for revealing His true identity to individuals, extending an invitation to anyone who was burdened and heavy laden. To all such who come to Jesus, He promised, "I will give you rest."

In the first century, the term *yoke* was used metaphorically for whatever controlled people's lives. Jesus' saying is made more vivid when we realize that in first-century Judaism the Law was spoken of as a yoke. Thus the daily repetition by the pious Israelite of the Shema (Deut. 6:4) was considered as submission to the divine law.

The Jewish rabbis also taught that there must be something which controls and gives direction to a person's life, and it was better that this be the divine law rather than man's law (the kingdom) or materialism (worldly care).

In contrast, Jesus offered another yoke: "My yoke." It is clear that this yoke was very different from the yoke of God's Law, especially as interpreted by the Pharisees of Jesus' day. Jesus' yoke was designed to lighten a person's heavy burden rather than to increase it. Jesus' yoke was designed to give the weary rest rather than to define another burdensome duty.

When Jesus' disciples ate grain on the Sabbath, the Pharisees condemned Christ's hungry followers (Matt. 12:1–8). Jesus then healed a man with a withered hand, and the Pharisees plotted to destroy Him. What a contrast these men of the Law were with Jesus, who explained that God was concerned with mercy and meeting human needs. No wonder Jesus' yoke was to be preferred to that of the Law as Israel interpreted it.

We find rest in claiming the mercy Jesus brings us in His cross. We also find rest in making mercy and grace controlling principles of our relationships with others.

—Larry Richards

GOD GIVES ME PEACE THAT SURPASSES UNDERSTANDING

"Be anxious for nothing, but in everything by prayer and supplication, with thanksgiving, let your requests be made known to God; and the peace of God, which surpasses all understanding, will guard your hearts and minds through Christ Jesus."

PHILIPPIANS 4:6, 7

In chapter 4 of Philippians, Paul offered exhortation and encouragement. He spoke from his own experience. Paul had been charged with a capital crime, and he waited in Rome for the verdict. In addition, Paul had a deep concern for the churches he had established in many cities of the Roman Empire. If any person had reason to be anxious, Paul did. And yet his letter conveys a sense of joy and peace—a peace whose secret he shares in Philippians 4.

Paul promised the "peace of God" would turn anxieties into prayers. The "peace of God" is a peace that God provides. It surpasses all understanding because it is not dependent on circumstances but on a relationship with the Lord. Christians and unbelievers alike face situations which create anxiety in most people. When this happens, our first impulse should be to turn the situation over to the Lord.

We claim this promise by committing ourselves and our problems into the loving hands of the God who loves us in Christ. We trust Him not only as a Father who cares for us, but as the sovereign Lord of the universe who is able and willing to meet our needs. As we turn the problem over to Him, God's Spirit ministers His peace to us. Our emotions and thoughts are calmed and quieted by God Himself.

It is one thing to know in an intellectual sense that God's protective love surrounds us. It is quite another matter to experience His protective love. The promise Paul shares here is that we will know through personal experience a peace that can come only from God.

—Larry Richards

GOD MAKES ME CONTENT WITH WHAT I HAVE

"And my God shall supply all your need according to His riches in glory by Christ Jesus."

PHILIPPIANS 4:19

The believers at Philippi had sent a gift of money to Paul while he was in prison. The word *prison* is deceptive. Paul was in Rome, awaiting trial. As a Roman citizen, Paul was not placed in a jail cell. He was under "house arrest." He was responsible for renting the house where he was staying and purchasing his own necessities. Since the apostle had no independent means of support, the money gift the Philippians sent must have met a real need.

So Paul thanked the Philippians for their generosity. He was particularly thankful for the concern that the gift reflected, and he called it "an acceptable sacrifice, well pleasing to God." God would reward the Philippian Christians, and this gave Paul joy.

Paul made this promise not for himself but for the Lord. The apostle had known times of plenty as well as destitution. He knew what it meant to be full as well as hungry. Through it all, God had been faithful.

The same God who had met Paul's needs many times would provide for the needs of His other children—even as He will meet our needs today.

This promise brings freedom, especially in a materialistic society, where people tend to seek meaning in things. Paul had learned that life cannot be measured in the abundance of things that we possess. In fact, Paul wrote, "I have learned in whatever state I am, to be content."

When we commit to the spiritual values that motivated Paul, we will also find a contentment that doesn't depend on our earthly possessions.

—*Larry Richards*

GOD PROVIDES A UNIVERSAL GOSPEL THAT INCLUDES ME

"That the Gentiles should be fellow heirs, of the same body, and partakers of His promise in Christ through the gospel."

EPHESIANS 3:6

The apostle Paul had identified a mystery (Eph. 3:3)—an unexpected element of God's plan which was not revealed in the Old Testament but which had now been made known in Christ. The mystery was the fact that Gentiles were to be "fellow-heirs" with Jews, and "of the same body."

The Old Testament made it clear that God had always intended to bless Gentiles as well as Jews (see. Is. 11:11; Jer. 16:19). Yet the Jews thought of themselves as having a closer relationship with God than the Gentiles could have. Gentiles would be blessed, the Jews agreed, but this blessing would come through Israel.

And then after the resurrection of Jesus, God's "promise in Christ" spread through the Roman world.

Old distinctions between Jew and Gentile became irrelevant as God formed a single body, the church, which included all people. In this body Gentiles were not subservient to the Jews but were fellow heirs, participating as equals in God's promise. Through Christ, God forms a bond of love between believers which breaks down barriers and makes us one.

Paul identified a cosmic purpose that God had in forming different people into one body. He said that God intended that "now the manifold wisdom of God might be made known by [through] the church to the principalities and powers in the heavenly places" (Eph. 3:10).

Paul was saying that the angels observe that the issues which once created hostility between groups of people are set aside in Christ. They notice as Christians live together in love as God's fellow-heirs. The angels are awed by the wisdom and greatness of God.

The world is also impressed when Christians live by the truth that we are one with our brothers and sisters in Christ, in spite of our differences.

—Larry Richards

GOD GRANTS ME ACCESS TO HIM THROUGH THE HOLY SPIRIT

"For through Him we both have access by one Spirit to the Father."

EPHESIANS 2:18

For thousands of years the human race was divided into Jew and non-Jew. The Jews, descendants of Abraham, had special access to God through the covenant promises made to Abraham and his descendants.

Then Jesus came. Through His death, He instituted the New Covenant that the prophet Jeremiah predicted would replace the Law. Under the New Covenant, the door of access to God was thrown open to all humanity. The old distinction between Jew and Gentile was done away with, and God formed "one new man" from what had been two.

The terms *Jew* and *Gentile* were made irrelevant when both became "Christian." Ephesians says that God reconciled them "both to God in one body through the cross" (Eph. 2:16). Both now have access to the Father by the one Holy Spirit.

The Greek word translated "access" in this passage is *prosagoge*. In oriental courts, the *prosagogeis* was the official who brought visitors into the king's presence. Thus, this verse identifies the Holy Spirit as one who conducts all Christians—whatever their ethnic origin—into the presence of God. As Christians, we have direct access to God's throne.

We claim this promise by exercising our right to enter God's presence. We come to Him in prayer—whether in praise, petition, intercession, or meditation on who He is. We should take joy from the privilege of visiting the Ruler of the universe.

The promise of access to God by the Spirit reminds us of an important reality: All of us are one in Christ. The distinctions so important to ordinary people—differences of race, education, social status, and wealth—are irrelevant to God. The relationship with Jesus that we share with all other believers makes us one. All other distinctions are unimportant.

—*Larry Richards*

GOD PROVIDES A MEDIATOR WHO CARES FOR ME

"For there is one God and one Mediator between God and men, the Man Christ Jesus."

1 TIMOTHY 2:5

We all want sympathy, so we readily tell friends our troubles, but faith teaches that there is no sympathy equal to that of Christ Jesus and no power the equal of our heavenly Father. Therefore, tell your troubles to your best Friend. Take your burdens to your Mediator, Jesus Christ, and unload them at the foot of the cross. With childlike reliance on His power, go to Jesus for help. Go without hesitation or delay.

This is a rule of God's providence, "Call upon Me in the day of trouble; I will deliver you, and you shall glorify Me" (Ps. 50:15). Rest assured that the Lord, who provides for the millions of fish in the sea and the myriads of birds in the air (Matt. 6:26) will not allow His children to perish. He who cares for the glow-worm on a damp bank and for a bug in the woods will never forsake His own (Ps. 94:14).

Whether your troubles are tangible or spiritual, leave them with God. Cry to Him in prayer. Walk in His fear and trust in His name, and sooner or later in one way or another He will make a way of escape. Other promises may turn out to be mere wind, but faithful is He who has promised. "He shall deliver you in six troubles, yes, in seven no evil shall touch you" (Job 5:19). You shall "dwell in the land, and feed on His faithfulness. Delight yourself also in the Lord, and He shall give you the desires of your heart" (Ps. 37:3, 4) "No good thing will He withhold from those who walk uprightly. O Lord of hosts, blessed is the man who trusts in You" (Ps. 84:11, 12).

We will be happy if we believe and act on this.

—*Charles Haddon Spurgeon*

JESUS PROVIDES ME A HELPER LIKE HIMSELF

"And I will pray the Father, and He will give you another Helper, that He may abide with you forever—the Spirit of truth, whom the world cannot receive, because it neither sees Him nor knows Him; but you know Him, for He dwells with you and will be in you."

JOHN 14:16, 17

The Holy Spirit is the third person of the Trinity, God with the Father and the Son. The identification of the Spirit as God is implicit in John's choice of the word that is translated "another." The Greek word *allos* means "another of the same kind," in contrast to *heteros*, another of a different kind.

Jesus told His disciples that He would no longer be present with them in a physical sense but that God would provide a Helper of the same kind: God the Spirit, who would take up the discipling ministry of God the Son. Jesus promised that the Holy Spirit would abide (stay) with His disciples forever, and that He would be *in* rather than *with* them.

Ever since the day of Pentecost, the Holy Spirit has been the permanent companion of the Christian. He is present now as our Helper. The New Testament names or describes a number of ministries of the Holy Spirit. These ministries of the Spirit helps us sense how important this promise was.

Jesus' promise of the Holy Spirit has been kept. The Spirit came to dwell within believers on the day of Pentecost (Acts 2). He is now present in everyone who has trusted Christ as Savior (1 Cor. 12:7; Rom. 8:9). Because the Holy Spirit is within us, we have immediate access today to all the power we need to live vital Christian lives.

—Larry Richards

GOD FILLS MY LIFE WITH THE FRUIT OF THE SPIRIT

"Walk in the Spirit, and you shall not fulfill the lust of the flesh."

GALATIANS 5:16

Paul had argued that a Christian is not under the law (Gal. 4) and must assert his or her freedom from the law. But won't such "freedom" lead to sin?

Paul's answer was to depict the Christian life as a struggle between the flesh and Spirit. The flesh is the source of such sins as "adultery, fornication, uncleanness, lewdness, idolatry, sorcery, hatred, contention, jealousies, outbursts of wrath, selfish ambitions, dissensions, heresies, envy, murders, drunkenness, revelries, and the like" (Gal. 5:19–21).

Opposed to the flesh is the Holy Spirit. The Spirit energizes the Christian's new nature to produce a totally different kind of fruit. The fruit produced by the Spirit is "love, joy, peace, longsuffering, kindness, goodness, faithfulness, gentleness, self-control" (Gal. 5:22, 23).

To "walk in the Spirit" means to be responsive to the leading of the Holy Spirit. As we take our cue from the Spirit and rely on Him, God promises that we will not fulfill the "lusts of the flesh." The Greek word for "lusts"refers to the motives, desires, and cravings of the sinful human nature. God does not promise that we will no longer feel sinful desires or crave sinful things after we become Christians.

He does promise that if we are responsive to the Holy Spirit in our daily walk, our lives will not be characterized by sin but by a very different fruit. When we produce the fruit of the Spirit, the law will be irrelevant.

God will not force us to live holy, happy lives. God's promise of a life in which sins find no room for expression is conditional. We choose between walking in the Spirit and responding to the prompting of our sin nature. When we choose to walk in the Spirit, we truly become free.

—*Larry Richards*

GOD HEARS AND ANSWERS MY PRAYERS

"And whatever things you ask in prayer, believing,
you will receive."

MATTHEW 21:22

Just the day before Jesus had cursed a fig tree, whose leaves promised a fruit it did not deliver. The disciples marveled, wondering how the tree could have withered so soon. Jesus told them that "if you have faith and do not doubt, you will not only do what was done to the fig tree, but also if you say to this mountain, 'Be removed and be cast into the sea,' it will be done" (Matt. 21:21). The prayer promise in Matthew 21:22 immediately followed this saying.

Jesus also used the image of the moving of a mountain in Matthew 17:20. The image is a metaphor of the humanly impossible—of a miracle that is possible only for God. Christ's point is that we have access through prayer to the supernatural, for the One to whom we pray is the God of miracles.

In verse 21 a tension is set up between faith and doubt. God's supernatural power is available to those who have faith and do not doubt.

Some people interpret this verse as "condition" for answered prayer. They reduce "belief" in Jesus to forcing ourselves to "believe" that God will do what we do not really believe He will do. Then, if our prayers are unanswered, the fault can be laid to our lack of faith!

In fact, this verse does not lay down a condition, but it commends a genuine trust in God and discernment of God's will. As we rest the full weight of our trust in God, seeking to know and do His will, our Lord's power will flow, and our prayers will be answered.

God calls us to trust Him and to seek His will in all things. As our discernment of God's will increases, we will pray with confidence, and our prayers *will* be answered.

—*Larry Richards*

GOD NOURISHES ME SPIRITUALLY

"Behold, I will rain bread from heaven for you."

EXODUS 16:4

The food that the Israelites brought from Egypt ran out before they reached Mt. Sinai. The people turned against Moses, accusing him and God of bringing them into the wilderness to kill them! God's response was to provide manna, a bread substitute, which appeared each morning except the Sabbath, and which continued to appear until the Israelites crossed into Canaan nearly forty years later.

Looking back on these years, Moses said, "So He humbled you, allowed you to hunger, and fed you with manna ... that He might make you know that man shall not live by bread alone; but man lives by every word that proceeds from the mouth of the Lord" (Deut. 8:3).

This promise was made to the Exodus generation. While unconditional, the promise was limited to the years the Israelites spent in the wilderness areas outside of Canaan. The experience was intended to teach Israel to rely completely on God. The Lord promised Moses that the manna would be supplied daily. Each day the people relearned the truth that they could depend on God's promise.

When Jesus was tempted by Satan, He quoted Deuteronomy 8:3 (see Matt. 4:4). Jesus would not act on Satan's suggestion but only on the Word of God. We should also look to God's Word for guidance in every situation.

Some time later Jesus fed a large crowd. They recalled God's provision of manna and wanted to make Jesus king. Christ refused. Israel had missed the message of the manna. While Christ was the true bread from heaven—God's provision for our spiritual lives rather than our biological needs—He must be appropriated by faith in God's Word about Him.

For us too, God's Word and spiritual blessings are to have priority. We are to love and serve God not because of what He can do for us, but because He is God.

—Larry Richards

JESUS CARES ABOUT MY MATERIAL NEEDS

"Then Jesus said to them, 'Children, have you any food?' They answered Him, 'No.'"

JOHN 21:5

During His days on earth, Jesus fed multitudes on two grand occasions (Matt. 14:13–21; 15:32–38). Now that He has died, is risen, and is in His glorified body, He still thinks of His people's hunger. He still calls, "Children, have you any food?" (John 21:5). Finding they have nothing, He says, "Come and eat breakfast" (John 21:12). These words fall graciously from His lips and prove His care for our earthly needs.

Our Lord and Savior is particularly mindful of the needs of His people. If you are needy and in difficult circumstances, be encouraged. He who said to His disciples, "Come and eat breakfast," will not forget you in your time of need. On your part, this is the time to exercise faith. On His part, now is the time for the display of His power.

If you look to friends, they may fail to help. So-called friends are far too ready to give the cold shoulder to those who are not well-to-do. But if you look to

God, your prayers will be answered. I cannot tell how, any more than I can tell how the Lord lighted that fire of coals or procured the fish that lay broiling on the fire, but there was the fire and there was the fish (John 21:9). The Lord provided. "Trust in the Lord, and do good; dwell in the land, and feed on His faithfulness. Delight yourself also in the Lord, and He shall give you the desires of your heart" (Ps. 37:3, 4)

He who taught you to say, "Give us this day our daily bread" (Matt. 6:11), did not teach an empty phrase. If your needs are so pressing as to make you hunger, look to Him for help. He is the same today as He was by the lake of Galilee.

—Charles Haddon Spurgeon

GOD GRANTS ME ETERNAL LIFE

"For God so loved the world that He gave His only begotten Son, that whoever believes in Him should not perish but have everlasting life."

JOHN 3:16

John 3:16, a part of Jesus' dialogue with a Pharisee named Nicodemus, has been called "the gospel in a nutshell." It establishes God's motive in sending His Son: love. It establishes the identity of Jesus: God's Son. It establishes God's goal in sending Jesus: to provide everlasting life to a perishing world. And it defines the promise implicit in Jesus' coming: whoever believes in Him will not perish but have everlasting life.

The word *believe* can be confusing. We believe that Augustus Caesar was the Roman emperor when Jesus was born. But there is a vast difference between this kind of belief and believing in the Jesus who lived in Augustus's time.

We believe what history tells us *about* Augustus. But we believe *in* Jesus Christ. What believing *in* means is that we *trust ourselves to* the Jesus of history.

We rely completely on Him and His sacrifice on Calvary. In doing so, we accept the gift of eternal life that He offers.

There's another difference too. Our beliefs about Augustus Caesar make no real difference in our lives. But our belief in Jesus Christ makes a profound difference. When we trust ourselves to Jesus, God enters our hearts and begins to work a wonderful transformation. Our motives and desires change, and with them our behavior changes also. Belief *in* Jesus initiates an inner transformation that gradually reshapes believers toward Jesus' likeness.

To claim God's promise of everlasting life, we must come to a conscious decision to rely on Jesus for forgiveness of our sins and accept God's wonderful gift of eternal life.

—*Larry Richards*

GOD GUARDS AND KEEPS ME

"'They shall be Mine,' says the Lord of hosts, 'On the day that I make them My jewels. And I will spare them as a man spares his own son who serves him.'"

MALACHI 3:17

There is a great depth of meaning in the word *keep*. A shepherd keeps sheep by feeding them, by supplying all their needs, and by guarding them from their adversaries. He vigilantly keeps the flock, so that it is not diminished by the ravaging wolf or the straying sheep. Night and day, even an ordinary shepherd takes the utmost care to preserve his sheep.

Our Lord Jesus, that great Shepherd of the sheep who was brought up from the dead (Heb. 13:20), uses His omnipotence, His omniscience, and His divine attributes to keep His sheep. Dear believer, rest assured, He will preserve you! You are in good keeping. He is the Shepherd, the great Shepherd and the chief Shepherd (1 Pet. 5:4).

The Lord keeps His people, not only as a shepherd keeps sheep, but also as a king keeps his jewels. These rare and precious gems are his special treasure, and he will not lose them. He will put them in a secure vault, and his most faithful servants will guard the place where they are stored. He will charge those who have the custody of the crown jewels to see that none are lost.

The Lord Jesus keeps His people the same way. They are His jewels. He delights in them, and they are His honor and His glory. They cost Him a greater price than can ever be realized. He hides them in the vault of His power and protects them with all His wisdom and strength.

Concerning those who trust in Him, it is written, "'They shall be Mine,' says the Lord of hosts, 'on the day that I make them My jewels'" (Mal. 3:17). God will never forget you.

—*Charles Haddon Spurgeon*

GOD IS MY SHIELD AND REWARD

"Do not be afraid, Abram. I am your shield, your
exceedingly great reward."

GENESIS 15:1

Abraham had just rescued his nephew Lot by defeat-
ing a raiding party. At first glance, the words "don't be
afraid" seem out of place. One would think that God
would speak them to encourage Abraham before the
battle was fought, not after it was won! But the verb *be*
afraid deals with the future. It invites Abraham to look
ahead and to dismiss future fears on the basis of the
victory God had just given him.

When God said "I am your shield," He was
expressing a proven reality. God's protection of His
servant is the explanation for Abraham's victory as
well as a promise of future protection.

While this promise was made specifically to
Abraham, it can be claimed by any believer. The reason is that the roots of the promise are not anchored in
who Abraham was, but in who God is for His own
people. The God who loved Abraham loves us. The

God who spread His protective wings over Abraham spreads them over us today.

We claim this promise by facing each day with renewed confidence that God is a shield around us. We claim it by choosing, as Abraham did, not to be distracted by material treasures from the true riches that are to be found in our relationship with the Lord.

We often find ourselves afraid to do something we know is right. What will others think? What do we risk if we choose to speak out? When we remember that God is a shield for His own people, we can set aside our fears and speak and act boldly for what is right. Nothing should distract us from a passionate desire to love God and glorify Him in all we do. When we make loving God our primary goal, we learn by personal experience how great is the reward we have in Him.

—*Larry Richards*

GOD GIVES ME MERCY AND GRACE IN TIMES OF NEED

"Let us therefore come boldly to the throne of grace, that we may obtain mercy and find grace to help in time of need."

HEBREWS 4:16

The old covenant had its high priest, who represented the people before the Lord, and who conveyed God's blessing to the people. Under the New Covenant, Jesus is our High Priest. Unlike the Mosaic Covenant's high priests, who ministered on earth as God's representatives and then died, Jesus has "passed through the heavens" and now sits with the Father on heaven's throne.

We are invited to "come boldly" to the throne of grace, aware that Jesus sympathizes with the pressures to which we human beings are subject. There, on his throne, we have a High Priest willing and able to provide what we need.

Christ subjected Himself to the limitations under which we live, with the exception that He never sinned. When we sin, we are invited to approach the throne of God with confidence, certain that we will obtain mercy from Jesus (see Eph. 2:4–5).

Grace in Scripture is the compassionate response of a person to help someone who is unable to help himself. While both mercy and grace flow out of compassion, the first is closely related to forgiveness while the second is more closely related to enabling. We appeal for mercy after failing; we seek "grace to help" to enable us to meet the challenges in our lives. When we come to the throne of grace seeking grace to help, Jesus will give us the strength we need to live godly lives.

Our cry of "help" reaches God's throne in the moment of our need. As soon as we sense failure, we can turn to Jesus for mercy; as soon as we feel overwhelmed or inadequate, we can appeal to Jesus for grace to help. And we can be sure that Jesus our High Priest will gladly supply what we need.

—*Larry Richards*

GOD WALKS WITH ME THROUGH THE FIRE

"When you pass through the waters, I will be with you; and through the rivers, they shall not overflow you. When you walk through the fire, you shall not be burned, nor shall the flame scorch you."

ISAIAH 43:2

These words were spoken to Israel as a people whom God created and formed, whom He redeemed, named, and chose to be His own (Is. 43:1). This litany clearly describes the covenant relationship which God established with Abraham and which He faithfully maintained through the millenniums.

Strikingly, each element of the relationship that God established with Israel is reflected in the Bible's picture of the Christian's relationship with God today.

Ephesians 2:10 says, "We are His workmanship, created in Christ Jesus for good works." First Peter 1:18, 19 says that we "were not redeemed with corruptible things, like silver or gold . . . but with the precious blood of Christ." Revelation 17:8 indicates that our names have been "written in the Book of Life from the foundation of the world." John 10:29 says that

Christians have been given to Jesus by the Father, "and no one is able to snatch them out of My Father's hand."

Relationship with God is no guarantee of an easy life. The promise implies that in the course of our lives we *will* pass through waters and walk through fire. Life will not treat us kindly simply because we belong to Jesus. We can lose our employment, be crippled in an automobile accident, contract cancer, see loved ones die.

What is different is that *when* we pass through the deepest waters or tread in the hottest fires, God is with us. The tragedies of our lives will test us, but they will not *harm* us. And during the time of greatest pain, we will sense the comforting presence of a God who stays with us, who feels our pain, and who will bring us safely through.

—Larry Richards

GOD SHELTERS ME FROM HIS WRATH

"He who believes in the Son has everlasting life; and he who does not believe the Son shall not see life, but the wrath of God abides on him."

JOHN 3:36

John in his Gospel reported Jesus' conversation with Nicodemus in which Christ presented the "gospel in a nutshell" (John 3:16). John had also quoted the testimony of John the Baptist about Jesus. In this verse the apostle John sums up the choice that faces each person: believe in Jesus and have everlasting life, or do not believe and face God's wrath.

We often think of promises as positive, welcome words. But in truth a promise is simply a commitment that a person makes to behave in a certain way. A father who says "If you're late, you'll be grounded" is no less making a promise than a father who says, "I'll be at your game tonight."

Thus this verse, which sets out the two choices given every person who hears of Jesus, is a promise. The promise is preceded by a simple statement. "He who believes . . . has everlasting life." There is no promise here for believers; none is needed. We have, now, as our present possession, eternal life.

No, the promise in this verse is a dread one. "He who does not believe the Son shall not see life, but the wrath of God abides on him." The person who does not believe has no hope. All that lies ahead for the unbeliever is an eternal experience of God's wrath.

Some people put off making a decision about Jesus, thinking they will make a commitment to Him in the future. But Scripture gives us only two choices. We either believe in Him, or we do not. "Later" is a choice not to believe.

If we truly believe God's promise of wrath ahead, we will decide for Jesus *now*.

—*Larry Richards*

GOD CARES FOR MY LOVED ONES

"Yet I will also make a nation of the son of the bond-woman, because he is your seed."

GENESIS 21:13

This verse is one of the clearest examples in Scripture of a personal promise. It grew out of a pain-filled situation as Abraham was compelled to give up his son Ishmael, whom he had fathered by Sarah's servant Hagar. It was accepted practice in Old Testament times for childless women to have their slaves serve as surrogates; children born to such slaves were considered to be children of the wife.

God fully understood all that Abraham was experiencing in this situation. Only the Lord could look ahead and tell what would become of the child whom Abraham loved but was about to lose. And God graciously shared His knowledge of the future with Abraham.

This promise shows that God's love reaches out, in some sense, to shelter our loved ones as well as us. The promise given to Abraham concerning Ishmael suggests that when we are forced to surrender our children, God

Himself takes over the parents' protective role. The promise reminds us that God not only cares for us; He also cares for those we love.

Too many families these days are torn apart by divorce. Some parents simply don't care about their offspring. But in many divorce cases, at least one parent is torn by the emotions that wracked Abraham as he contemplated the loss of his son. While the predictive element of the promise given to Abraham was made to him alone, the concern that God expressed reveals His heart of concern for everyone.

If we should ever find ourselves in the position of Abraham, we can respond to God's promise by trusting our children into His hands. We should remember that it is through our lives that our children first perceive the love and grace of God. And we can live our faith in Him before our children.

—*Larry Richards*

GOD PROTECTS ME FROM THE EVIL ONE

"But the Lord is faithful, who will establish you and guard you from the evil one."

2 THESSALONIANS 3:3

Some believers in Thessalonica thought the Second Coming had already occurred and that they had missed it! In chapter 2 of his second letter to the Thessalonian believers, Paul reminded them of his earlier teaching. He had told them that certain things would take place before Jesus returned. A world ruler—the "man of sin," the Antichrist—would appear and assume political power. Satan himself would support this evil ruler with signs (miracles) and "lying wonders."

Until then, Paul urged the Thessalonian Christians to stand firm and "hold the traditions which you were taught." As they waited for these events to take place, the Thessalonian Christians could be confident that the Lord was faithful and would guard them from the evil one.

This promise is one of inner security and of outward protection. The Greek word translated as *protect* is a military term, used of defense against a violent onslaught. Satan may hurl his forces against the believer, but our faithful Lord will provide a defense against him.

The military imagery is suggestive. Some Christians seem to live in fear of real and imagined enemies, retreating to fortified enclaves where they associate only with other Christians with similar convictions. But our true defense is the Lord, and He is with us always.

As believers, we may feel secure in every situation. We need to remember Jesus' words to the Father, "I do not pray that You should take them out of the world, but that You should keep them from the evil one" (John 17:15). Jesus also prayed, "As You sent Me into the world, I also have sent them into the world" (John 17:18).

God has promised to guard us from the evil one. He expects us to trust Him and to step out into the world as His representatives.

—*Larry Richards*

GOD CALMS MY FEARS

*"Do not fear, little flock, for it is your Father's good
pleasure to give you the kingdom."*

LUKE 12:32

Do you believe anything is left to chance? Is there any
event outside the circle of divine predestination? No,
my friend, with God there are no contingencies. The
mighty Charioteer of Providence has gathered the
reins of all the horses, and He guides them according
to His infallible wisdom.

Foreknowledge and predestination are in everything, from the motion of a grain of dust to a flaming
comet blazing across the sky. The Lord said, "Behold, I
have created the blacksmith who blows the coals in the
fire . . . and I have created the spoiler to destroy"
(Is. 54:16). The most violent people could not move a
finger if the Lord did not lend them strength.

As for nature's catastrophes, the Lord is distinctly
in them. "He shakes the earth out of its place" (Job
9:6). "He removes the mountains" (Job 9:5). Our Father
works all things! Why then should His children be
afraid? Regardless of how awesome events may be, we
know that nothing can happen to shake the kingdom

of God. Even the gates of Hades shall not prevail against that kingdom (Matt. 16:18). Our chief possession lies there, and if that is secure then all is safe. Our highest, best, and most vital interests are beyond even the shadow of harm. "Do not fear."

Suppose an accident should take our lives. I smile as I think that the worst thing that could happen would be the best thing that could happen. If we should die, we shall be with the Lord (1 Thess. 4:17). So, if the worst that can befall is the best that can come, why should we fear?

This is good reasoning. If you are a believer, and if God is your refuge, there is no logical reason to fear.

—*Charles Haddon Spurgeon*

GOD WILL WATCH OVER ME WHEN I AM OLD

"Even to your old age, I am He, and even to gray hairs
I will carry you! I have made, and I will bear; even I
will carry, and will deliver you."

ISAIAH 46:4

We are poor fools when we begin to deal with the
future. It is a sea that we are not called to navigate.
The present is the whole of life. When we enter the
future, it is the present.

Still, some of you worry as you feel infirmities
coming on. "What will I do when I come to extreme
old age? My friends will be gone, and I will have no
one to support me. When these fingers cannot work,
when my brow is wrinkled and I can scarcely totter to
my toil, what will I do?

Ah! "His mercy endures forever" (Ps. 136:1). It does
not stop at seventy or pause at eighty. It will carry you
safely over ninety if your pilgrimage is prolonged.

The other day I visited a number of elderly people
in a nursing home. Some had not been able to leave
their bed in years, and I thought it far better to die
than to live like that. But I was wrong. If Christ should

make that bed as soft as downy pillows with His presence, there might be a glory in the nursing home and a heaven in the midst of poverty. They would learn that even in a nursing home, "His mercy endures."

You whose days of weakness are coming, trust in the Lord and do not be afraid. He will not fail you. He will not forsake you.

—*Charles Haddon Spurgeon*

GOD TAKES AWAY MY FEAR OF DEATH

"And when I saw Him, I fell at His feet as dead. But He laid His right hand on me, saying to me, 'Do not be afraid; I am the First and the Last.'"

REVELATION 1:17

This "do not be afraid" may be specifically applied to the grave. We need not fear death, because Jesus has the key to the grave. Jesus will come to our dying bed in all His glory and say, Come with me "until the day breaks and the shadows flee away" (Song 4:6). The sight of Jesus as He thrusts in the key and opens that gate of death will make you forget the terrors of the grave.

Since Jesus has the sepulcher's key, never fear it again. Your dying hour will be the best hour you have ever known. Better than the day of your birth will be the day of your death. It will be the beginning of heaven, the rising of a sun that will never go down. Let the fear of death be banished by faith in a living Savior.

We have stood and peered as best we could through the mist that gathers over the black river. We have wondered what it must be like to have left the body and be flitting through that land from which no traveler has ever returned.

You do not pass from one province of your Lord's empire to another. In that spirit-land above, they speak the same language, the language of New Jerusalem, which you have already begun to speak. They acknowledge the King that you obey here. When you enter heaven, you will find them singing the praise of the same glorious One whom you adore. You will find them triumphing in the love of Him who was your Savior here below.

—*Charles Haddon Spurgeon*

GOD WILL TAKE ME TO
BE WITH HIM AFTER I DIE

"We are confident, yes, well pleased rather to be
absent from the body and to be present with the Lord."

2 CORINTHIANS 5:8

The time is coming when we will die unless the Lord descends from heaven with a shout (1 Thess. 4:16). "Yea though I walk through the valley of the shadow of death, I will fear no evil; for You are with me; Your rod and your staff, they comfort me" (Ps. 23:4).

Death is delicious to God's people because Jesus is near. Through death we escape death. It is not death to die. When Jesus meets His saints, the iron gate is passed through, for in a moment the believers close their eyes on earth and open them in glory. Beloved, you should not fear death. Christ is with His people on their bed of weakness and even in their descent to the grave. This has been a great joy to many departing saints.

Attended by a believing physician, a dying saint was whispering, so the physician placed his ear against the dying man's lips and heard these words again and again, "Present with the Lord, present with the Lord, present with the Lord" (2 Cor. 5:8). When heart and flesh were failing, the departing one knew that God was the strength of his life and portion. So he chose for his soft, low, dying song, "Present with the Lord."

"We are confident, yes, well pleased rather to be absent from the body and to be present with the Lord" (2 Cor. 5:8):

> Death may my soul divide
>
> From this abode of clay;
>
> But love shall keep me near Thy side
>
> Through all the gloomy way.

—*Charles Haddon Spurgeon*

GOD HEARS ME IN MY TIME OF TROUBLE

"Call upon Me in the day of trouble; I will deliver you, and you shall glorify Me."

PSALM 50:15

Oh Lord, You see how great my trouble is! It is heavy. I cannot carry it, and I cannot get rid of it. It follows me to bed, and it will not let me sleep. When I rise, it is still with me. I cannot shake it off. My trouble is unusual. Few are as afflicted as I am. Please give me extraordinary help, for my trouble is crushing. If you do not help, I will soon be broken! This is good reasoning and good pleading.

Turn your adversity to advantage. Go to the Lord this moment and say, "Lord, do you hear me? You have commanded me to pray. I, though I am evil, would not tell anyone to ask me for something unless I intended to honor his request. I would not urge them to ask for help if I meant to refuse it."

When God tells you to call on Him, He will deal compassionately with you. You are not urged to pray in the hour of trouble to experience deeper disappointment. God knows that you have trouble enough without the added burden of unanswered prayer. The Lord will not unnecessarily add even a quarter of an ounce to your burden. When He tells you to call on Him, you may call on Him without fear of failure.

So speak reverently, but with belief, "Lord, it is You Yourself to whom I appeal. You said, 'Call upon Me in the day of trouble; I will deliver you' (Ps. 50:15). So Lord, by Your truth, by Your faithfulness, by Your immutability, and by Your love, I call on You in the day of trouble. Help me soon, or else I die."

If I were in trouble, I would pray like David, Elijah, or Daniel in the power of this promise.

—*Charles Haddon Spurgeon*

GOD DELIVERS ME FROM SELF-PITY

"But he himself went a day's journey into the wilderness, and came and sat down under a broom tree. And he prayed that he might die, and said, 'It is enough! Now, Lord, take my life, for I am no better than my fathers!'"

1 KINGS 19:4

It is difficult for a young person to understand why Elijah could be so dreadfully depressed as to pray, "It is enough! Now, Lord, take my life" (1 Kin. 19:4). As we grow older and more experienced, our trials multiply and our inner life enters difficult conflicts. Then we come to understand why God allowed His servants to be put in these situations. There is relief in discovering that we are walking paths that others have traveled.

We understand Elijah's attitude on Mount Carmel when he said, "I alone am left" (1 Kin. 18:22), and we comprehend why he executed the prophets of Baal (1 Kin. 18:40). If we are puzzled about why he got under a juniper bush (1 Kin. 19:4) or hid in a cave (1 Kin. 19:13), we understand the reasons when we ourselves get under the juniper and remember that Elijah once sat there.

When we hide in a cave, it is a comfort to remember that this great prophet also did.

Perhaps you have prayed Elijah's prayer. One saint's experience is instructive to others. Many of the psalms—called Maschil, or instructive psalms—record the writer's experiences and become our textbooks.

Remember that God has such blessings in store for you that your mouth will be filled with laughter and your tongue with singing. The Lord has done great things for you, and you will be glad (Ps. 126:2, 3). Be of good courage. Strengthen your heart and wait on the Lord until He comes. May His blessing be with you forever!

—Charles Haddon Spurgeon

GOD DELIVERS ME FROM SATAN'S POWER

"Resist the devil and he will flee from you."

JAMES 4:7B

The Bible depicts Satan as a powerful fallen angel, who is hostile to humankind. He is particularly malicious toward those who trust in the Lord and is eager to harm them.

While he is powerful beyond our ability to imagine, Satan is a defeated enemy. Christ "disarmed" all demonic powers on the cross, "triumphing over them in it" (Col. 2:15). As believers, we are in Christ and we share in His victory.

The promise that when we resist the devil he will flee from us is preceded by a call to "submit to God" (James 4:7a). We are not able to resist Satan in our own strength, nor should we try to do so. The secret of resisting Satan is to first submit to God, so that His power flows through us. When we are submitted to God, we are in the center of His will, relying completely on Him. When we enjoy this relationship with the Lord, Satan can do nothing but flee.

Christians are to have a healthy respect for Satan. This will keep us from rushing into spiritual conflicts for which we are not prepared. In the prayer that Jesus taught His disciples, one request was, "Deliver us from the evil one" (Luke 11:4).

On the other hand, some Christians credit Satan with too much power. Rather than resist Satan, they run from him and avoid spiritual warfare. Our fear of Satan can be just as harmful as overconfidence.

The balance is found in submitting daily to the Lord, making Him the focus of our faith. Then if Satan should trouble us, we can meet his challenge with confidence, resisting in the power of the Lord.

—Larry Richards

God Gives Me Victory
over Temptation

"No temptation has overtaken you except such as is common to man; but God is faithful, who will not allow you to be tempted beyond what you are able, but with the temptation will also make the way of escape, that you may be able to bear it."

1 Corinthians 10:13

God is true to His promises. "God is faithful, who will not allow you to be tempted beyond what you are able" (1 Cor. 10:13). "God is faithful," and He will fulfill that promise. "My sheep hear My voice, and I know them, and they follow Me. And I give them eternal life, and they shall never perish; neither shall anyone snatch them out of My hand" (John 10:27, 28). "God is faithful," and God will fulfill these promises.

You have often heard this promise, "As your days, so shall your strength be" (Deut. 33:25). Do you believe it? Or will you make God a liar? If you believe it, then banish all dark depression with this blessed little sentence, "God is faithful."

God sends our trials at the right time. If He puts an extra burden on us in one way, He takes something off in another. John Bradford, the famous martyr, suffered with rheumatism and depression. Yet when they imprisoned him in a foul damp dungeon, and he knew that he would never come out except to die, Bradford wrote, "It is a singular thing that ever since I have been in this prison and have had other trials to bear, I have had no touch of my rheumatism or depression."

How blessed, and you will find that this is true, "God is faithful, who will not allow you to be tempted beyond what you are able, but with the temptation will also make the way of escape, that you may be able to bear it" (1 Cor. 10:13).

—*Charles Haddon Spurgeon*

GOD GRANTS ME FREEDOM THROUGH HIS TRUTH

"If you abide in My word, you are My disciples indeed. And you shall know the truth, and the truth shall make you free."

JOHN 8:31, 32

This statement appears in a passage that described a heated conflict. Jesus warned some Pharisees that if they did not believe, they would die in their sins (John 8:13–29). He also stated that the physical descent from Abraham which they considered important was actually meaningless (John 8:33–59). The lengthy confrontation concluded with Jesus' assertion that He was the "I AM"—the Yahweh of the Old Testament whom the Pharisees claimed to worship as God.

According to Jesus, believers must "abide in My word." The phrase means to live in accord with, to keep, or to obey Jesus' word. What benefit does abiding in Jesus' word bring? Those who abide in Jesus' words will "know the truth," and this will "make you free." In John, "to know" means "to know by personal experience." When we live by Jesus' words, we learn the truth of what Jesus taught by personally experiencing what His words reveal.

People tend to think of "freedom" as license to do whatever they want to do when they want to do it. But in Scripture, freedom is far different. Freedom is a release from that which holds man in bondage. Freedom is extrication from the inner drives which pull toward what is wrong and harmful. Freedom is emancipation from all that prevents us from becoming our true and ideal self.

To find this kind of freedom, we surrender what we want to do in favor of choosing what God wants us to do. When we make this daily surrender and commit ourselves to keeping Jesus' words, we discover that Jesus truly does free us and make us whole.

—*Larry Richards*

GOD TRANSFORMS MY LIFE THROUGH HIS SPIRIT

"But if the Spirit of Him who raised Jesus from the dead dwells in you, He who raised Christ from the dead will also give life to your mortal bodies through His Spirit who dwells in you."

ROMANS 8:11

In Romans 7 the apostle Paul shared his own experience as a believer eager to please God. Because he truly wanted to please God, he struggled to keep God's Law. But the harder he tried, the more conscious he became that something within him reacted against the Law, perverting even his most valiant efforts.

All of us have experienced this frustration. We want to sing a solo to the glory of God. But even as we praise Him, we find something deep within hoping the congregation will be impressed by our voice. Like Paul, we discover that the harder we try to live righteous lives, the more we become aware of the corrupting taint of sin.

To understand this promise, we need to understand the relationship between the Law and the heart. Many people assume that when the Law says, "Love your neighbor," what God requires is that we help neighbors and refrain from harming them. But the real problem pointed out by the Law is that the human heart is corrupt. A person intent on keeping the Law can perform the actions that the Law defines. But the Law cannot transform the heart so that the acts are true expressions of love. Apart from an inner transformation, our best efforts to keep the Law will fall short.

We are not called to live under the Law, measuring each action against its rules and regulations. We are called to surrender ourselves to His Holy Spirit. The Spirit who raised Jesus raises us as well, transforming us from within. As we respond to the Spirit's prompting, we find ourselves living truly righteous lives.

—*Larry Richards*

GOD MINISTERS TO ME THROUGH DIVINE MESSENGERS

"Behold, I send an Angel before you to keep you in the way and to bring you into the place which I have prepared."

EXODUS 23:20

God through Moses gave Israel laws to live by when they possessed the land of Canaan (cf. Ex. 23). How could Israel, then in the Sinai wilderness, know they would possess the land? God promised to send an angel before them, to protect and to aid. (See also Ex. 32:34; 33:2.)

The promise of divine aid is followed immediately by a warning not to disobey the Lord. The generation to which this promise was made later refused to attack Canaan when God commanded them to do so (see Num. 14). As a result, all in that generation except two, Joshua and Caleb, died in the wilderness. Some 38 years later their descendants, who were obedient, did enter and conquer Canaan. Yet the promise which the first generation to leave Egypt failed to claim remained good. And it was claimed by their children. God remained faithful in spite of His people's unfaithfulness.

This promise of aid was given specifically to ancient Israel and related to the conquest of Canaan. At the same time, the incident gives us insight into the ministry of angels to believers of every era. Angels are described in the Bible as "ministering spirits sent forth to minister for those who will inherit salvation" (Heb. 1:14). They help us today even as they aided ancient Israel.

Perhaps the most wonderful lesson contained in the passage is that God's promises remain open. The Exodus generation failed to obey God, and the promise was not fulfilled for them. Their children did obey God, and God's angel brought them into the promised land (cf. Judg. 2:1). Although disobedience may keep us from claiming a promised blessing at one time in our lives, when we return to the Lord we may find that the promise is still ours to claim.

—*Larry Richards*

GOD RAISES UP OTHERS TO SHARE MY BURDENS

"I will take of the Spirit that is upon you and will put the same upon them; and they shall bear the burden of the people with you, that you may not bear it yourself alone."

NUMBERS 11:17

In spite of God's miracles on behalf of the Israelites, the Exodus generation continued to grumble and complain. Moses was driven to despair, his leadership an affliction rather than a blessing! God responded by. promising Moses that He would give others the Spirit, that they might share the burden of leadership with Moses. The promise was fulfilled when God anointed seventy elders of Israel (Num. 11:24–25).

Earlier at Sinai Moses had followed the advice of his father-in-law Jethro and established a series of courts (Ex. 18:13–23). These courts dealt with lesser disputes, allowing Moses to deal only with the most difficult cases. The specific responsibilities of the seventy mentioned here are not defined. But it is clear that God's endowment of them with the Spirit equipped them to share leadership with Moses.

The incident introduces a principle reflected in both testaments. While God has raised up individuals to lead the nation Israel and to serve the whole church, leadership in the communities of ancient Israel and in local congregations of New Testament times was provided by teams of elders. The people of faith are not to be lorded over by autocrats. They are a community guided by elders who share responsibility and spiritual authority. God will put His Spirit upon members of such teams so they may bear the burden of leadership together.

The promise made to Moses established a pattern which we are to follow. God expects no one to bear the burden of leadership alone. In every setting—from the family to the church—we are to share with partners the responsibilities and authority of leadership.

—Larry Richards

GOD GRANTS ME INNER PEACE

"These things I have spoken to you, that in Me you may have peace. In the world you will have tribulation; but be of good cheer, I have overcome the world."

JOHN 16:33

This verse concluded John's account of Jesus' words to His disciples the night before He was crucified. A major theme of Jesus' teaching that night was God's provision of the Holy Spirit as a Comforter who would come to the disciples after Jesus' departure. Christ's concluding promise of peace summed up all He had taught His followers.

Jesus' promise reminds us that we can choose to live our lives in one of two realms. We can live "in the world" and be ruled by the values and passions that dominate human society. Or we can live "in Christ" and be ruled by the desire to do the will of God.

There are two senses in which we have tribulation "in the world." First, we live in a culture shaped by humankind's sinful passions. It is not surprising that a person who seeks to live by God's will should be buffeted by tribulation in a society that is essentially hostile to God. But second, we may have tribulation because we adopt the values and passions of the world. If we do this, we will have tribulation indeed, for there is nothing in this world which can satisfy the human heart.

Christ calls us to live in Him. When we adopt Jesus' values and way of life, other people may trouble us. But by choosing to live our lives in Jesus, we will find an inner peace and wholeness that escapes those who are "of the world." What we experience is the peace that Jesus knew, even in the face of rejection by His own people. We will experience a peace rooted in the knowledge that Jesus in His death and resurrection has overcome the world.

—Larry Richards

God Goes into Battle on My Behalf

"You will not need to fight in this battle. Position yourselves, stand still, and see the salvation of the Lord, who is with you, O Judah and Jerusalem."

2 Chronicles 20:17

Jehoshaphat was one of Judah's godly kings. When a coalition army of Moabites and Ammonites attacked Judah, Jehoshaphat turned to God and called on his people to fast and pray. In his prayer, Jehoshaphat honored God by expressing confidence in His ability to save. He also claimed the promise the Lord had made to Solomon to hear the prayers of those who appealed to Him at His temple. Jehoshaphat then appealed to God to judge the enemy. God then sent a messenger to the king with His promise, along with instructions to "go down against them" the next morning.

Jehoshaphat and the people worshiped and praised the Lord and marched out of the city. When they reached a rocky overlook, they saw the bodies of the enemy spread across the valley. The Ammonites and Moabites had turned on each other, and all that was left for the Jews to do was collect the spoil. Like other fulfilled promises in the Bible, this one testifies to the faithfulness of God.

What is most impressive about this story is the response of king and people to God's promise. They worshiped, praised God, and the next morning marched out to battle still singing praises. How often we remain skeptical until a promise is fulfilled. To these Israelites, promise and fulfillment were one. They rejoiced in the promise given as we often rejoice in the fulfillment.

To honor God, we need to view His promises as Jehoshaphat did. We are to rejoice in God's promises and act on them, assured that God's promises *will* be fulfilled.

—*Larry Richards*

GOD GUIDES ME LIKE A SHEPHERD

"The Lord is my shepherd; I shall not want."

PSALM 23:1

Give me ten million dollars, and one reversal of fortune may scatter it. Give me a spiritual hold on the divine assurance that "the Lord is my Shepherd; I shall not want" (Ps. 23:1), and I am set for life. I cannot go broke with this stock in my hand. I can never be bankrupt with this security.

Do not give me ready cash; give me a checkbook and let me withdraw what I need. This is how God works with the believer. God does not immediately transfer the inheritance; He lets us draw what we need out of the riches of His fullness in Christ Jesus. "The Lord is my Shepherd; I shall not want." What a glorious inheritance! Walk up and down it. Rest on it. It will be a soft downy pillow for you to lie on.

Climb the creaking staircase of your house, lie down on your hard mattress, wrap yourself in a blanket, and look out for the winter of hard times. But do not say, "What shall I do?" Just hum, "The Lord is my Shepherd; I shall not want." This will be the hush of a lullaby to your soul, and you will soon sleep peacefully.

Business people, go to your office and review your wearisome books. You say, "How about my business? These prices will ruin me. What can I do?" Analyze your accounts and enter this against your fears: "The Lord is my Shepherd; I shall not want." Write that in your checkbook. It is better than gold and silver.

If you disregard this truth—"The Lord is my shepherd; I shall not want"—you know nothing about its preciousness. If you grasp it, you will find this promise is like Chianti wine, which the ancients said flavored the lips of those who tasted it.

—*Charles Haddon Spurgeon*

GOD GIVES ME ACCESS TO THE MIND OF CHRIST

"I will raise up for them a Prophet like you from among their brethren, and will put My words in His mouth, and He shall speak to them all that I command Him."

DEUTERONOMY 18:18

God commanded the Israelites not to look to any of the occult practices engaged in by the surrounding nations when seeking guidance. God knows that situations will arise in which the nation or individuals will need special guidance not available through the written Word. He promises to guide in these situations— through prophets whom He will raise up.

This promise has dual reference. As the capitalization of "He" in Deuteronomy 18:15 and 18 indicates, the passage refers to a particular prophet whom God would send to Israel. This is a reference to the Messiah.

This promise also implies the sending of other spokesmen whom God would send His people in time of need. The Old Testament tells about many prophets whom God raised up for Israel. These prophets advised kings, confronted sin, and interpreted current events in the light of God's covenants.

Should we take this job, or that? Should we marry, or wait? Should we send our children to a private or a public school? Questions like these call for special guidance. And God still guides us, though not through prophets. God has given us the Holy Spirit as a leader and guide (John 16:13; Gal. 5:18). He will show us God's will as we look to Him today.

As the Israelites were to consult prophets when seeking God's guidance, so we are to turn to the Holy Spirit. Neither prophets nor the Spirit will lead us to violate the written Word of God (cf. Deut. 13:1–5). Through the Holy Spirit we have access to the mind of Christ, who guides His own even today (1 Cor. 2:16).

—*Larry Richards*

GOD FILLS ME WITH HIS WISDOM

"If any of you lacks wisdom, let him ask of God, who gives to all liberally and without reproach, and it will be given to him."

JAMES 1:5

Wisdom involves the application of spiritual truth to daily life, so that we sense the godly thing to do in any situation. This promise of wisdom is a promise of divine guidance. If you don't know what to do in a situation, ask God. He doesn't get upset with us for asking—no matter how minor the thing that concerns us. Instead, He will surely give us wisdom when we ask for it.

This is one of those wonderful promises that we should claim each day. The more we desire to do those things that please the Lord, the more we will become aware of the "little" daily decisions that are essential elements in living godly lives. As we look to the Lord for guidance, He will show us what to do.

James gave us a warning with this promise (1:6–8). To receive guidance, we must "ask in faith" with no "doubting." What James means by "doubting" is explained by his image of a person tossed by the waves and his description of that person as "double-minded." The person of faith is determined to do God's will when it is revealed to him. This person will be given the divine guidance he asks for.

On the other hand, the double-minded person who doubts is uncertain about his readiness to do God's will. He wants to stand in judgment on God's directives. We are not to pray, "Lord, show me what to do, and if I like it, I'll do it." That kind of prayer will not be answered. What we must pray is, "Lord, show me your will, and I'll obey, no matter what."

When we ask God for wisdom with this single-minded attitude, He will provide the guidance we need.

—*Larry Richards*

GOD HELPS ME MAKE TOUGH DECISIONS

"Now the Lord came and stood and called as at other times, 'Samuel! Samuel!' And Samuel answered, 'Speak, for Your servant hears.'"

1 SAMUEL 3:10

Perhaps you are facing a tough decision. You may not know which of two opportunities to choose. Some friends have urged you to follow one plan and some have urged you to follow the other. If you have used your best judgment and have tried to direct your steps according to the Word of God, you will receive an answer. God will give you distinct guidance.

Take your difficulty to the God of wisdom and spread your situation before Him. Divest your own will and solemnly desire to know God's will. Then expect to have an answer from the Most High. Make your prayer the one that the boy Samuel prayed: "Speak, Lord, for Your servant hears."

We need to acknowledge the Lord in the common transactions of daily living. If we do not, we may, like the Israelites with the Gibeonites, be betrayed in the

simplest transaction and deceived to our lasting injury
(2 Sam. 21:9).

"Lord, direct us" is a good prayer for the citizens of
heaven. This is my advice: Take your difficulty to God
in prayer and say, "Speak, Lord, for Your servant
hears." Do not ask God to confirm your opinion; ask
Him to make your opinion conform to His truth.

Follow the simple Word of God as you find it. Let
the Holy Spirit flow on the sacred page, and as you
read you will hear the Master say, "This is My Word."
He will make it come to your soul with power. You
will have no doubt when your heart cries, "Speak,
Lord, for Your servant hears."

—*Charles Haddon Spurgeon*

GOD WORKS WITH ME TO RESOLVE CONFLICTS

*"Assuredly, I say to you, whatever you bind on earth
will be bound in heaven, and whatever you loose on
earth will be loosed in heaven."*

MATTHEW 18:18

According to Jesus, what should we do if a person sins against us? We should go to him alone (Matt. 18:15). If he does not hear, we should take others with us and try to be reconciled again (Matt. 18:16). If he refuses to listen, we should bring the matter to the church (Matt. 18:17). If he refuses even then to work toward a resolution of the conflict, he is to become "like a heathen and a tax collector" (i.e., cut off from fellowship).

Jesus assured believers that in using this community process, their joint action would be confirmed in heaven. In following this process, believers will be doing heaven's will, and the outcome of following the process will be guided and confirmed by God Himself.

This promise is made to the believing community. It is an especially precious promise, as we tend to draw back from confrontation, hoping that hurts and the damage caused by interpersonal sins will "go away."

Jesus reminds us that the impact of such sins on the believing community is serious and should be addressed. God's promise that He will be involved in the process is great encouragement, especially when we remember that the goal of the process is not punishment but the restoration of harmony and fellowship (cf. 2 Cor. 2:5–8 with 1 Cor. 5:1–5).

Is there someone who has hurt you deeply enough to block the flow of mutual love between you? We can experience God in the process of reconciliation if we take the steps which Jesus outlined in this passage.

—*Larry Richards*

GOD HELPS ME TO DISCERN HIS WILL

"If anyone wills to do His will, he shall know concerning the doctrine, whether it is from God or whether I speak on My own authority."

JOHN 7:17

Opposition to Jesus by the religious leaders finally hardened to the point where they planned to kill Him. Yet when Jesus showed up in Jerusalem in the middle of the week-long tabernacles festival and began to teach, the Jews [a phrase which John uses to refer to religious leaders, not the race] were frustrated by His evident knowledge of the Scriptures.

Christ initiated a challenge by stating, "My doctrine [teaching] is not Mine, but His who sent Me." He continued to express His challenge by identifying the source of their hostility. A person committed to do God's will would know that Jesus' teaching was from God. Clearly then, the leaders' failure to acknowledge the authenticity of Jesus' teaching was rooted in their failure to submit to God and their unwillingness to do His will.

There is an implicit promise in Jesus' statement. Christ located the issue of recognizing truth not in the intellect but in the heart. If there is a readiness to do God's will, discernment follows.

While Jesus' words were addressed to the skeptics of His day, they have application to us today. God wants us to know Him, and to understand both His revelation and His will for our lives. Our ability to discern both truth and God's daily guidance hinges not so much on our intellect as on our heart attitude. If we are committed to doing God's will, whatever that will may be, we will be able to discern God's will.

—*Larry Richards*

GOD INFLUENCES ME THROUGH GODLY ROLE MODELS

"The things which you learned and received and heard and saw in me, these do, and the God of peace will be with you."

PHILIPPIANS 4:9

God is the source of peace for believers. But there is more to living in a state of peace than turning to God when we are under stress. A second element in Paul's prescription is to keep our thoughts focused on those things that promote godliness. We are to think on "whatever things are noble, whatever things are just, whatever things are pure, whatever things are lovely, whatever things are of good report"—the virtuous and the praiseworthy (Phil. 4:8).

Another way to experience God's peace is to live the Christian life as Paul has taught and modeled it. Paul's personal ministry and his letters provided instruction in Christian living. These were the things which the Philippians "learned and received." But Paul did more than instruct in Christian living. He modeled it in his own life. Thus the Philippians "heard and saw" the gospel enfleshed "in me." The outcome of this modeling was that the Philippians might "do" as Paul instructed. They were to follow Paul's instruction and example.

How important this is. Only when we *do* the Christian life do we experience the God of peace.

To claim this promise, we must take some initiative. Today the apostle Paul still instructs us in Christian living through his letters in the New Testament. But we must look for models of the Christian life elsewhere as well. We can never underestimate the importance of building close personal relationships with committed Christians who can serve as models of Christian commitment. We can also serve as examples for others.

As we "do" what we learn and receive from Scripture and hear and see these principles enfleshed in God's people, the God of peace will fill our lives.

—*Larry Richards*

GOD GUIDES ME INTO HIS REST

"Therefore, since a promise remains of entering His rest, let us fear lest any of you seem to have come short of it. . . . There remains therefore a rest for the people of God."

HEBREWS 4:1, 9

When God declared that "there remains a rest for the people of God," He invited us to experience the same peace and certainty about the future that He Himself enjoys. How is this possible?

The writer of Hebrews reminded us that "the word of God is living and powerful, and sharper than any two-edged sword, piercing even to the division of soul and spirit, and of joints and marrow, and is a discerner of the thoughts and intents of the heart" (Heb. 4:12). That is, God knows us totally.

"All things are naked and open to the eyes of Him to whom we must give an account" (Heb. 4:13). We have no pain or no need that God does not understand completely. And the God who is master of history is intimately involved in our lives! Even as God has planned for every cosmic contingency from the time of creation, so God has planned how to meet every need of ours from the very beginning of time. The rest which we are offered is a rest found in trusting God to know what is best for us, and following His leading. It is clear that this promise is contingent, for Hebrews urges "Let us therefore be diligent to enter that rest" (Heb. 4:11).

When we grasp the teaching of this passage, we gain a wonderful new perspective on Christian living. God, who knows our every need and has already planned for every contingency in our lives, will guide us. He will speak to us every day. When we hear His voice, all we need do is obey. We find our rest in trusting and responding to God's voice as He guides.

—*Larry Richards*

GOD INSTRUCTS ME THROUGH HIS SPIRIT

"The Lord, before whom I walk, will send His angel
with you and prosper your way, and you shall take a
wife for my son from my family and from my father's
house."

GENESIS 24:40

When it was time for Abraham's son Isaac to marry, Abraham sent a servant to arrange a marriage within his extended family. The servant expressed concern that no young woman would be willing to leave her home to travel hundreds of miles to marry a man she had never seen. Then Abraham told him that God would "send His angel before you" (Gen. 24:7).

When the servant arrived in Haran, where Abraham's relatives lived, God answered the prayer for guidance and showed the servant His choice for Isaac's bride: Rebekah.

The experience of the servant raises a significant issue. No inferred promise has the credibility of a promise expressed in God's Word. We should hesitate before claiming a promise inferred by anyone.

At the same time, Abraham was a man of faith who walked with God. It may well be that the Holy Spirit speaks in the hearts of those who walk with God and that silent promises which we can count on do pass between God and man.

The apostle Paul asked, "Who has known the mind of the Lord that he may instruct Him?" Then Paul added, "But we have the mind of Christ" (1 Cor. 2:16). God has in the Spirit given us access to the mind of Christ! As we walk with God, His Spirit may breathe special promises into our hearts.

The gift of God's Spirit enables us to evaluate situations for ourselves and to sense the Spirit's direction. In cases of such private leading, we are not to judge others. And when we sense God's leading in our lives, we are not to let others dissuade us from what we believe to be God's will.

—*Larry Richards*

GOD GUIDES ME INTO ALL TRUTH

"However, when He, the Spirit of truth, has come, He will guide you into all truth; for He will not speak on His own authority, but whatever He hears He will speak; and He will tell you things to come."

JOHN 16:13

This promise is misunderstood by some people. They argue that since sincere Christians differ on various points of doctrine, this promise has failed. First, of course, there has been and still is a common core of beliefs subscribed to by all true Christians. Second, Jesus did not promise that the Spirit would lead all Christians to agree doctrinally. Jesus promised that the Spirit would guide believers in *the way of all truth.*

Earlier Jesus had told those who believed in Him that they would "know the truth" and that the truth would set them free (John 8:31, 32). "Knowing the truth" means *experiencing* truth by putting Jesus' teachings into practice. In John 16:13, Jesus was speaking of the same thing—experiencing God's truth. Thus, the Holy Spirit is charged with the ministry of guiding believers into an experience of the truth revealed in

Jesus. The Holy Spirit is not charged with leading all Christians to agree on every point of doctrine.

How wonderful it is that God has sent His Spirit to guide us in the way of all truth. And how we need to rely on the Spirit each day of our lives. We need His wisdom so we might understand how God's truth relates to every aspect of our lives. And we need the strength He provides to enable us to walk in God's ways.

The promised Holy Spirit has come. He continues to speak within our hearts, showing us the way that we are to walk in Jesus' truth. We need only to reach out, relying on God's Spirit to provide the guidance we need.

—*Larry Richards*

GOD GIVES ME HOPE IN A HOPELESS SITUATION

"So the man of God said, 'Where did it fall?' And he showed him the place. So he cut off a stick, and threw it in there; and he made the iron float."

2 KINGS 6:6

The borrowed axe head was hopelessly lost underwater. The honor of the prophetic band was threatened because the name of their God would be compromised. Against all expectations, the iron rose from the stream's bed and floated when the prophet Elisha cut a stick and threw it into the water. "The things which are impossible with men are possible with God" (Luke 18:27).

A few years ago a Christian I knew was assigned to a project that far exceeded his ability. It was so difficult that the very idea of attempting it bordered on the absurd. Yet he was told to do it, and his faith rose to the occasion. God honored that faith, and unexpected aid was sent: the iron floated.

Another member of the Lord's family was in a disastrous financial situation. He would be able to meet all of his obligations and much more if he could sell part of his estate. When it did not sell, he was placed under great pressure. In vain he sought the help of friends, but then faith led him to the unfailing Helper and the trouble was averted. "God enlarged his path under him, so his feet did not slip" (2 Sam. 22:37). The iron floated.

Beloved, what is your desperate problem? What heavy trial hangs over you? Bring it to the mercy seat. The God of the prophets lives. He lives to help His saints, "that you may lack nothing" (1 Thess. 4:12). Believe in the Lord of hosts! Approach Him. Plead the name of Jesus. The iron will float.

—*Charles Haddon Spurgeon*

GOD STRENGTHENS ME TO DO HIS WORK

"What then shall we say to these things? If God is for us, who can be against us?"

ROMANS 8:31

You may assume that those of us who are always before the public speaking of the blessed promises of God are never downcast or heartbroken. You are mistaken. We have been there, and perhaps we know how to say a word in season to any who are now going through similar experiences. With many enterprises on my hands, far too great for my own unaided strength, I am often driven to fall on this promise of my God, "I will never leave you nor forsake you" (Heb. 13:5).

If I feel that any plan has been of my devising, or that I sought my own honor, then I know that the plan must fail. But when I can prove that God has thrust it on me, how can my God forsake me? How is it possible for Him to send His servant to battle and not comfort him with reinforcements when the battle goes hard? God will never desert any of His servants.

If the Lord calls you to things you cannot do, He will give you the strength to do them. If He should push you still further, until your difficulties increase and your burdens become heavy, "as your days, so shall your strength be" (Deut. 33:25). You shall march with the indomitable spirit of those who have tried and trusted the arm of the eternal God.

"If God is for us, who can be against us?" Though earth, hell, and all their crew come against you, if the God of Jacob stands at your back, you will thresh them as though they were wheat and drive them as though they were chaff. Roll this promise under your tongue. It is a sweet food.

—*Charles Haddon Spurgeon*

GOD ENABLES ME TO RESIST TEMPTATION

"No temptation has overtaken you except such as is common to man; but God is faithful, who will not allow you to be tempted beyond what you are able, but with the temptation will also make the way of escape, that you may be able to bear it."

1 CORINTHIANS 10:13

God does not exempt any believer from temptation. Nor does God intervene to keep us from surrendering to our temptations. Rather, God makes it possible for us not to surrender to temptation by providing "the way of escape."

A temptation is not a sin in itself (James 1:12). In fact, temptations can be a source of blessing, because we are strengthened spiritually when we successfully resist them. James argued that we are to see situations in which we are tempted as a good gift from God, through which He intends us to be blessed rather than overcome (James 1:13–17).

As Christians, we never face our temptations alone. We have a relationship with a faithful God, who is with us and who never permits us to be tempted beyond what we are able to bear. Simply put, we do not *have* to give in. We are called to master our temptations—not to be mastered by them.

Too often temptations are treated as playthings. We keep them around to entertain us, pretending that we have no intention of giving in. This is no way to escape the corrupting influence of the temptations that are common to human beings. God's prescription for escaping our temptations is to escape them by getting away from them.

God's promise about temptations is conditioned on our readiness to acknowledge temptations and to avoid them as much as possible.

—*Larry Richards*

GOD GIVES ME HIS FAVOR

"And Jabez called on the God of Israel saying, 'Oh, that You would bless me indeed, and enlarge my territory, that Your hand would be with me, and that You would keep me from evil, that I may not cause pain!' So God granted him what he requested."

1 CHRONICLES 4:10

Jabez prayed for more land and greater responsibility. The desire for wealth is so universal that it is almost a natural instinct. Have you ever thought that if you were wealthy you would indeed be blessed? There are ten thousand proofs that wealth does not bring happiness. Some people with easy circumstances have uneasy minds. Those who have acquired all they could wish for have been dissatisfied because they did not have more.

Frequently, wealth defrauds its owners. Delicious food is placed on the table, but the appetite fails; musicians give private concerts, but the ears are deaf; vacations are unlimited, but recreation has lost its charm. Perusing pleasure can become more burdensome than work.

If you are wealthy you may well say, "My God, let me continue to eat husks. Let me never make a god of silver and gold, goods and chattel, estates and investments, all of which in Your providence You have given. 'Oh, that You would bless me indeed, and enlarge my territory, that Your hand would be with me' (1 Chr. 4:10). As for these worldly possessions, they will be my destruction unless I have grace with them."

If you are not wealthy—and perhaps most of you will never be—say, "My Father, You have denied me this outward and seemingly good wealth. But enrich me with Your love. Give me the gold of Your favor, and bless me indeed. Allot to others whatever You will. Divide my portion, and my soul will wait Your daily direction. Bless me, and I will be content."

—*Charles Haddon Spurgeon*

GOD GIVES ME PATIENCE UNDER PERSECUTION

"My brethren, count it all joy when you fall into various trials."

JAMES 1:2

Think of the priceless virtue that is produced by various trials: patience! We all have a large supply of it until we need it, and then we have none. The person who truly possesses patience is a person who has been tested.

What kind of patience do we get from the grace of God? It is a patience that accepts the trial as from God. Calm resignation does not come at once. Often, long years of physical pain, or mental depression, or career disappointment, or multiple deaths are needed to bring the soul into full submission to the Lord's will. After much crying, the child is weaned. After much chastening, the son is made obedient to the Father's will. By degrees, we learn to end our quarrels with God and to desire that there be not two wills between God and ourselves but one, that God's will may be our will.

Patience enables us to bear ill-treatment, slander, and injury without resentment. We feel it keenly, but bear it meekly. Like our Master, we do not open our mouths to reply; we refuse to return shout for shout. We give blessing in return for cursing, like the sandalwood tree that perfumes the axe that cuts it.

"Love suffers long and is kind; love does not envy; love does not parade itself, is not puffed up; does not behave rudely, does not seek its own, is not provoked, thinks no evil; does not rejoice in iniquity, but rejoices in the truth; bears all things, believes all things, hopes all things, endures all things. Love never fails" (1 Cor. 13:4–8). If the grace of God by trial will work this in you, then you have gained a solid weight of character.

—*Charles Haddon Spurgeon*

GOD IS MY HELPER WHO NEVER FAILS

"So we may boldly say: 'The Lord is my helper; I will not fear. What can man do to me?'"

The fact that the Lord has constantly been our helper confirms our faith. If in looking back we could find a point where God failed, we might let our faith waiver. I speak from experience. I cannot find one example in all my life in which God was untrue or unkind. If we never doubt God until we have a reason, we will never doubt so long as we live.

Yesterday I looked at some birds in a cage. These poor little creatures are entirely dependent on those who feed them. They cannot help themselves. If seed and water are not supplied, they will die. Yet there they sit and sing with all their might. Their state of dependence never bothers them. They never think that their keeper will fail them.

I am God's singing bird. Perhaps I wonder where I shall get my bread or my next sermons, and a great many cares and troubles come to me. But why should I be troubled? Instead of mistrusting my keeper, who

— 1 2 0 —

has fed me these many years, I had best sit and sing as loudly as I can. That is the best thing to do. The birds do it, so why not us? We are suppose to have more intellect than a bird, but at times we do not seem to have half as much.

The Lord has constantly been true. Do not doubt. If some remarkable trial should come upon you between here and heaven, you will find deliverance from Him who has been your helper. "For He Himself has said, 'I will never leave you nor forsake you.' So we may boldly say: 'The Lord is my helper; I will not fear'" (Heb. 13:6).

—*Charles Haddon Spurgeon*

GOD REFINES ME IN THE FURNACE OF AFFLICTION

"Behold, I have refined you, but not as silver; I have tested you in the furnace of affliction."

ISAIAH 48:10

God's people are opposed by the current of the times, just as their Master was. It will cost sorrow and tears if you fully follow your Master. We are little of what we should be until the Lord puts us on the anvil and uses the hammer. He is doing that now with some of you. Do not complain. Let the soft whisper of this promise sustain you, "I have tested you in the furnace of affliction" (Is. 48:10).

You have struggled hard to rise out of your situation, but as often as you have striven you have fallen back to your hard lot. Do not be depressed. Live in your calling with contentment, because the Lord has said, "I have tested you in the furnace of affliction."

Merchant, your firm is going to pieces, and you will be poor. But you have faith in God. It is the Lord's will that you should struggle. He says, "I have tested you in the furnace of affliction."

Mother, you have lost a little one, and another is sick, so you say, "I cannot bear it." But you will bear it, for the Lord says, "I have tested you in the furnace of affliction."

Are you alone? Weep no more. The Lord loves you when no one else does. He says, "I have tested you in the furnace of affliction."

Some of you are like ferns. You only flourish in the damp and in the shade; too much sunlight would not be good. Your Master knows that if He put you where you would like to be, it would be deadly. Thus He writes, "I have tested you in the furnace of affliction."

—*Charles Haddon Spurgeon*

GOD HELPS ME COPE
WITH PAIN AND SORROW

*"But he said to her, 'You speak as one of the foolish
women speaks. Shall we indeed accept good from God,
and shall we not accept adversity?' In all this Job did
not sin with his lips."*

JOB 2:10

Our memory of God's goodness is often crushed by
pain. When we suffer sharp pain, or weary aches, or a
high fever, we tend to forget the days of health and
strength. We only remember the sharp intervals of
weakness and sorrow.

When we stand over the grave of a loved one, we
are likely in the loss to forget the loan. When a dear
one is taken, a precious loan has been called by its
Owner. We ought to be grateful to have been allowed
to borrow the comfort. We should not complain when
the Owner takes what He kindly lent.

When these loved ones are gone, do not look at
their going, but thank God that we had them. Bless a
taking and a giving God, who only takes what He
gave. We live too much in the present. We dwell on the
troubles of today and forget the Lord's mercy.

Perhaps you are growing old and feeble, and you cannot do what you once did. But bless the Lord for your years of vigor. Your mind is weak, but bless God that there was a time when you could serve Him without fatigue.

Perhaps your funds are low and you are afraid of poverty. Be grateful that you have had enough for many long years. Perhaps you are now sad. Recall the days when you praised the Lord on the high-sounding cymbals and stood on the high places of earth. Do not let memory fail because of the present crushing sorrow. May the Holy Spirit help your infirmities and bring His lovingkindness from past years to your memory.

—*Charles Haddon Spurgeon*

GOD STRENGTHENS MY FAITH THROUGH AFFLICTION

"Before I was afflicted I went astray, but now I keep Your word."

PSALM 119:67

The way to a stronger faith usually lies along the path of sorrow. Only as faith is contested will faith be confirmed. I do not know if my experience is similar to all of God's people, but all the grace I have received in comfortable and easy times could lie on a penny. The good that I have received from sorrow, grief, and pain is incalculable.

What do I not owe to the hammer and the anvil, the fire and the file? What do I not owe to the crucible and the furnace, the bellows that flamed the coals and the hand that thrust me into the heat? We may wisely rejoice in various trials, knowing that the testing of our faith produces patience (James 1:2–3). And through this we are exceedingly enriched and our faith grows strong.

An old Puritan said that if you go into the woods and are very quiet, you will not know whether there is a partridge, or a pheasant, or a rabbit in it. But when you move or make a noise, you soon see the living creatures. When affliction comes into your soul and makes a disturbance and breaks your peace, your graces rise. Faith comes out of hiding and love leaps from its secret place.

A bird's nest is hard to find in the summer, but anyone can find one in the winter. When all the leaves are off the trees the nest is highly visible. Often in prosperity, we fail to find our faith. Yet when adversity comes, the winter of our trial bares the branches, and we immediately see our faith.

"Before I was afflicted I went astray," said David, "but now I keep Your word." He found that his faith was there when he kept God's Word in the time of affliction.

—*Charles Haddon Spurgeon*

GOD MAKES ME STRONGER THROUGH DIVINE DISCIPLINE

*"Now no chastening seems to be joyful for the present,
but painful; nevertheless, afterward it yields the
peaceable fruit of righteousness to those who have
been trained by it."*

HEBREWS 12:11

Hebrews 12 is Scripture's classic passage on divine discipline. It encourages us to understand when trials or suffering come that God is not punishing us, nor has He deserted us. Instead, God is treating us as a loving Father, who wants to guide us toward maturity. God's discipline is training that produces righteousness.

In Hebrews 12:12–17, the author gave some practical advice on our response to God's discipline.

"Strengthen the hands which hang down" (*Heb. 12:12*). This image is one of hopelessness. The person gives up. His head rests on his chest, his hands hang down at his side, and his knees almost give way. The word *strengthen* tells us that we should resolve to keep on rather than give up.

"Make straight paths" (*Heb. 12:13*). We generally try to avoid the difficulties that God brings into our lives in order to mature us. Rather than run away from painful experiences, we need to move on through them.

"Fall short of the grace of God" (*Heb. 12:15*). One of the dangers of our times of trouble or suffering is that we might "fall short of the grace of God." This phrase is explained in the contrasting phrase that follows: "lest any root of bitterness springing up cause trouble."

More than one person undergoing divine discipline has become bitter, feeling that the treatment is unfair. But even our most painful experiences are gracious gifts of a loving Father, who intends to bless us rather than harm us.

What a wonderful thing it is to experience grace in times of suffering. How strengthening it is to realize that everything that happens to us is a gift from the God of love.

—*Larry Richards*

GOD OFFERS ME FORGIVENESS AND HEALING THROUGH HIS GRACE

"If My people who are called by My name will humble themselves, and pray and seek My face, and turn from their wicked ways, then I will hear from heaven, and will forgive their sin and heal their land."

2 CHRONICLES 7:14

Solomon dedicated the temple at Jerusalem that he had constructed in honor of the Lord. At the dedication, Solomon asked God to be available to His people, so that should they pray at or toward the temple, God would hear and answer. God would not "live" in the temple (1 Kin. 8:27). But the temple would serve as a place of meeting where sacrifices and prayers could be presented to God.

The promise of available grace was made to all God's people. They could come to God with their requests. But they could not expect Him to bless them while they pursued wicked ways. God is always ready to forgive. But He cannot be taken advantage of or treated with disrespect.

God is a forgiving God, always ready to restore us. His eyes are open and His ears are attentive to our prayers. Yet God is God, and if we are to know His richest blessings we must be committed to Him.

The writer of Hebrews restated the ancient promise, with one significant change. Israel approached God by coming to the temple. The Christian comes boldly to the very throne of grace in heaven (Heb. 4:16). The Hebrews verse tells us that at God's throne we "may obtain mercy and find grace to help in time of need." The forgiveness promised Israel is always available to us. And in addition there is grace, that in our time of need we might find strength to remain faithful to the Lord.

—*Larry Richards*

GOD HEALS MY
TENDENCY TO WANDER
AWAY FROM HIM

"Return, you backsliding children, and I will heal your backslidings."

JEREMIAH 3:22

Jeremiah 3 is an extended appeal to the people of Judah to return to the God who loves them. Woven into the invitation is a reminder of the Abrahamic and Davidic promises concerning their national future. But the fate of the people of Jeremiah's time depended on their response to the Lord.

There is an urgency to Jeremiah's words. The future of God's people is assured. But their fate depended on their willingness to return—now—to the Lord.

It is so easy to backslide. The tendency to sin is always with us. Even King David, who was known for his commitment to the Lord, committed adultery with Bathsheba in a moment of weakness. Then he compounded his sin by having her warrior husband sent to the front lines so he would be killed (see 2 Sam.

11:1–17). Only God has the power to heal our tendency to wander away from Him and His will for our lives.

We hear a lot these days about addictions. There is addiction to drugs, tobacco, alcohol, sex, and gambling. Anyone in the grip of one of these addictions knows how powerful its pull is. A whole "recovery" literature has been developed to help those with addictions and their families. One principle of most recovery programs is to urge the addict to rely on a "higher power."

Scripture personalizes this principle, presenting a God who is Creator and Redeemer, and who alone is able to heal our backsliding. The steps which recovery programs offer can be helpful. But ultimately only God can do in our lives what He promised to do for Israel when Jeremiah announced, "I will heal your backslidings."

—*Larry Richards*

GOD LIFTS ME UP IN TIMES OF DEPRESSION

"But he himself went a day's journey into the wilderness, and came and sat down under a broom tree. And he prayed that he might die, and said, 'It is enough! Now, Lord, take my life, for I am no better than my fathers!'"

1 KINGS 19:4

It may be that I am speaking to a sad person who is suffering from mental depression. This verse shows that the prophet Elijah had a problem with this condition. After he had killed the prophets of Baal, he fled from Jezebel into the wilderness, where he fell into a deep state of depression.

I have sometimes envied those good people who are never excited with joy and consequently are seldom or ever depressed. At the same time, when I rise as with eagle's wings in joyful rapture, I feel glad to be capable of the blissful excitement. Yet if you soar to the skies, you are apt to drop below sea level. He who can fly, can fall.

If you are one of those plants that seldom bloom with bunches of bright flowers, but if you have blossoms hidden and concealed, do not be uneasy. If you are never happy and seldom able to call yourself joyful, the only cure for your depression is faith.

Settle this in your heart. Whether you are up or down, the Lord Jesus Christ is the same. Whether you sing or sigh, the promise is true and the Promiser is faithful. Whether you stand on Tabor's summit or are hidden in the vale of Baca, the covenant stands firm and everlasting love remains.

Believe in Him, though you see no flashes of delight or sparkles of joy. You are safe because you are in the City of Refuge and not because you are healthy or ill. If you will stand firm in Christ Jesus, even in your weakness you will be made strong.

—*Charles Haddon Spurgeon*

GOD HEALS MY BROKEN HEART

*"The Lord is near to those who have a broken heart,
and saves such as have a contrite spirit."*

PSALM 34:18

Many people in this world live with broken hearts. A broken limb of any kind is bad; bruised and wounded flesh is hard to bear. But when you heart is crushed or broken, or when your spirit trembles, you are depressed and utterly wretched. You are dreary company. Other people get away from you like the herd leaves the wounded deer to bleed and die alone. People instinctively avoid the company of those who are habitually gloomy. Their own desire for happiness leads people to escape from the miserable.

Those who are taught by God will help the brokenhearted, but human sympathy is soon worn out because of its inability to help. You can set a limb and the bone will grow, but what can you do with a broken or crushed heart? Not liking to attempt the impossible and not caring to be continually baffled, it seems natural even to good people to avoid the depressed. Thus, the sad are doomed to sigh, "Loved one and friend You have put far from me, and my acquaintances into darkness" (Ps. 88:18).

When people comfort the depressed, they often become bitter by their conscious failures. They criticize until the poor tortured creature cries out in agony, "Miserable comforters are you all!" (Job 16:2). The trials of the brokenhearted are difficult because they are often despised and avoided.

Happy is it for them that "the Lord is near to those who have a broken heart, and saves such as have a contrite spirit" (Ps. 34:18).

—*Charles Haddon Spurgeon*

GOD RESTORES MY
FALTERING FAITH

*"Call to Me, and I will answer you, and show you
great and mighty things, which you do not know."*

JEREMIAH 33:3

This promise was addressed to the two fallen Hebrew
kingdoms. Israel had fallen long before Jeremiah
prophesied. Jerusalem and Judah were about to be
crushed by the Babylonians as a divine punishment.
Yet even as judgment threatened to fall, God spoke to
His people and invited them to call on Him. What
"great and mighty things" will the Lord do when His
people call on Him? God said through Jeremiah, "I
will bring it [Jerusalem] health and healing; I will heal
them and reveal to them the abundance of peace and
truth" (Jer. 33:6).

The prospect of a complete restoration of God's
people to their land is rooted in the Abrahamic
Covenant and the New Covenant. Because God had
promised, the descendants of Abraham would build a
lasting nation in what was ancient Canaan. But this
promise tells us more of *when* this will happen. One

day God's people will call on Him. When they do, God will answer with great and mighty acts.

The covenant-linked promise was made to God's Old Testament people. Yet it speaks powerfully of God's universal mercy and grace. When things are darkest in our own lives, God is the one on whom we can call with confidence. He not only cares, but He has the ability to do great and mighty things for us.

To claim this promise, we need only remember who God is and then call on Him. We cannot begin to know beforehand what great and mighty things He will do for us. But we need only know that He will. He who will bring a dead nation back to life is surely able to breathe life into our dead hopes.

—*Larry Richards*

THE GOD OF PEACE FILLS MY LIFE WITH PEACE

"Now may the Lord of peace Himself give you peace always in every way. The Lord be with you all."

2 THESSALONIANS 3:16

These words are inexpressibly sweet. If you think for a moment, you will see that we never obtain peace except from the Lord. In your trials, what will bring peace? Let me tell you, the Lord of peace Himself. I find great peace thinking about His mysterious person. He is a Man, "tempted as we are, yet without sin" (Heb. 4:15). A Man who knows every grief of the soul and every pain of the body—thus His tender sympathy and power to deliver. His person is a source of peace.

Rest in your soul by meditating on His death. View Him wounded, bleeding, and dying on the cross. A wonderful calm will steal over your heart. Jesus is that bundle of myrrh and spice (Song 5:1) from which peace flows like a sweet perfume. When He comes near your heart and shows you His wounds and speaks His love, you feel the divine fervency of His peace. When He assures you that you are one with

Him, united in an everlasting embrace that knows no divorce, your soul is steeped in peace.

This is an experiential business, and words cannot express it fully. "The Lord of peace Himself give you peace always in every way. The Lord be with you" (2 Thess. 3:16). He does not just offer peace, or argue that you ought to have it, or only show the grounds for it. He gives it. He can give you peace. He will give you peace.

—*Charles Haddon Spurgeon*

GOD RESTORES MY LOSSES

"And the Lord restored Job's losses when he prayed for his friends. Indeed the Lord gave Job twice as much as he had before."

JOB 42:10

Many people think that God has a great deal to do with their prayer closet but nothing to do with their pantry. If this were so, life would be dreadful. We should see as much of the Lord's hand on the kitchen table as on the communion table. The same love that spreads the table when we commemorate our Savior's dying love also spreads the table to provide our daily bread. Learn to praise God for all you have.

It may be that you have suffered a financial loss. Dear friend, the Lord can restore your loss. Although Job lost everything, God eventually restored his losses (Job 42:10). "Yes," you say, "but that was a remarkable case." But we have a remarkable God, and He still works wonders.

Consider the matter, for it was remarkable. Job lost all his property. It was equally remarkable that he got it all back. Surely, if God can scatter, He can gather. If

God could scatter Job's large holdings, He could, with equal ease, restore it.

We see God's destructive power. We do not, however, always see His building power. Yet it is more consistent with God's nature to give and not to take. It is more like Him to caress rather than to chastise.

It was a strange work of God to take all of Job's property and bring him to deep distress. But when the Lord again enriched Job, He was doing what He delights to do. God's happiness is most clearly seen when He is distributing the bounty of His love.

Can you look at your own circumstances in this light? It is more likely that God will bless and restore rather than chasten. He can restore your wealth, your health, and even more.

—*Charles Haddon Spurgeon*

GOD GRANTS HEALING THROUGH THE POWER OF PRAYER

"The prayer of faith will save the sick, and the Lord will raise him up. And if he has committed sins, he will be forgiven."

JAMES 5:15

The question of healing divides Christians. Some are convinced that every human ill can be cured with enough faith. This approach is sometimes carried to an extreme. Some children have died of curable diseases because their parents refused to seek medical treatment.

While it is clear that God sometimes heals persons miraculously, most Christians believe that prayer should be accompanied by medical treatment. Most also believe that healing is dependent on God—not on the faith of the person who prays or the individual who is sick.

James's topic was not sickness, but prayer and the power of prayer. What did James promise? Are all our diseases to give way to prayer? Is good health a Christian heritage, to be claimed by faith?

Note that the prayer James calls for is corporate rather than individual prayer. The phrase "prayer of faith" focuses our attention on God rather than on those praying. The efficacy of prayer does not depend on the amount of faith we have, but on the One in whom we place our trust. James follows up the promise of healing with a reference to Elijah, whose prayers shut off and then restored rain. If the prayers of Elijah, a man like ourselves, affected the course of nature so drastically, we must believe in the efficacy of prayer.

How important it is to be part of a believing fellowship of Christians who have confidence in God and believe in the power of prayer. When sickness comes, we can call on the leaders of our church to pray for us and ask our Christian brothers and sisters to join in as well.

—*Larry Richards*

GOD REPLACES MY WEAKNESS WITH HIS STRENGTH

"Even the youths shall faint and be weary, and the young men shall utterly fall, but those who wait on the Lord shall renew their strength; they shall mount up with wings like eagles, they shall run and not be weary, they shall walk and not faint."

ISAIAH 40:30, 31

With Isaiah 40 the tone of this great prophecy changes. Earlier chapters were colored by the threat of impending judgment. Now, suddenly, a note of joy is introduced which will echo throughout the rest of the book. God loves His chosen people and holds their future in His hand.

This exquisite passage expresses one of Scripture's universal promises. The promise is not made to a specific individual or relegated to a specific time. This is a promise made to all who "wait on the Lord."

If we want to claim this promise, there is one condition we must meet. We must be weak and "have no might." The person who is confident of his or her ability will never experience the blessing offered here. The person who relies on his talents will soon reach the limit of these natural gifts and fail.

This is one of the great paradoxes of our faith. To be strong, we must be weak. To soar, we must faint. Only when we give up can we succeed. We must rely so completely on God that whatever we accomplish is clearly His work and not our own.

What these verses promise is that when we do acknowledge our weakness, and turn to Him, God will provide us with His strength. When we rely on Him in our exhaustion, He enables us to run and not be weary. When our last resources are gone, He enables us to walk on. Only in our weakness can we experience the fullness of His strength.

—*Larry Richards*

GOD CREATED ME FOR FELLOWSHIP WITH HIM

"So God created man in His own image; in the image of God He created him; male and female He created them."

GENESIS 1:27

What a wonderful promise is implicit in the declaration, "God created man in His own image." Human beings, created in God's image, have a value and significance far greater than anything else in God's universe! Each person's life is precious beyond measure.

This image-likeness is best understood as personhood—the sum of those qualities that made both God and human beings persons. Like God, we human beings can appreciate beauty. We can find satisfaction in meaningful work, can invent and create, can think and remember, and can make moral choices.

What is most significant, however, is that in sharing His image-likeness, God made it possible for human beings to have a personal relationship with Him. In creating us in His image, God lifted human beings far beyond the animal realm. His gift of image-likeness carries a promise of personal relationship with Him.

Many people today have a low self-image, a sense of worthlessness. But every human being is actually a person of worth and value, because God created us in His image. We are special, gifted with unique capacities that make it possible for us to succeed in this world and to have a personal relationship with God.

On a personal level, God's promise in Genesis 1:26 is to shape our sense of personal worth and value. A low self-image is simply not appropriate for any person who bears the image-likeness of God.

On an interpersonal level, we are to respond to the promise of significance by treating others as God sees them—as persons of worth and value. When we view people in this way, we begin to grasp how important it is to give every person the respect he or she deserves and to be concerned about their needs.

—Larry Richards

GOD LOVES ME WITH AN EVERLASTING LOVE

"The Lord has appeared of old to me, saying: 'Yes, I have loved you with an everlasting love; therefore with lovingkindness I have drawn you.'"

JEREMIAH 31:3

Can our heavenly Father be unkind? "Oh give thanks to the Lord, for He is good! For His mercy endures forever" (Ps. 136:1). His name, His essence, is love, and "His mercy endures forever." He is the unchangeable God, the one "with whom there is no variation or shadow of turning" (James 1:17).

Heirs of heaven, can you believe that God is indifferent to His children? "If you then, being evil, know how to give good gifts to your children, how much more will your heavenly Father give the Holy Spirit to those who ask Him!" (Luke 11:13).

Have you ever felt that you would joyfully take your child's pain to relieve her suffering? Do you think that as a poor, fallen creature you have love and compassion, but that your heavenly Father has none? You may say with the prophet Jeremiah, "This I recall to mind, therefore I have hope. Through the Lord's mercies we are not consumed, because His compassions fail not. They are new every morning; great is Your faithfulness" (Lam. 3:21–23). Remember these verses, and know that the Lord cannot be careless about your welfare.

The eternal God loves you and chose you before the foundation of the world (Eph. 1:4). The snow-capped mountains are newborn babies compared with his love for you. He chose you! He might have passed you by, but He chose you to be His own. Jeremiah says, "The Lord has appeared of old to me saying, 'Yes, I have loved you with an everlasting love; therefore with lovingkindness I have drawn you'" (Jer. 31:3).

—*Charles Haddon Spurgeon*

GOD INCLUDES ME IN HIS SALVATION PLAN

"And I, if I am lifted up from the earth, will draw all peoples to Myself."

JOHN 12:32

The crisis point of Jesus' ministry had arrived, as reflected in His contemplation of His coming death (John 12:23–27). When some Greeks approached one of Christ's disciples with the request to see Jesus, He turned them away. That was not the time, although the time would come soon enough.

The "if I am lifted up" in this promise should be understood as "when I am lifted up." The expression *lifted up* has a dual reference. First, it refers to the cross (John 12:33). But the Greek preposition *ek* means "out from" the earth, and not merely away from it. Thus, Jesus' words about being lifted up also imply His resurrection and exaltation to God's right hand.

Shortly after making this statement, Jesus was lifted up—first on the cross and then to heaven itself after His resurrection. Thus, the condition Jesus stated had been met, and the promise "I will draw all peoples to Myself" was now in force.

Some scholars have suggested that this promise was Jesus' true response to the request of the Greeks. For His promise was that the gospel message would be addressed to all peoples, without reference to race or nationality. Through His cross and resurrection, Jesus even now draws all people to Him.

The fact that the gospel is for all people places a special obligation on Christians. If the gospel is for all, it must be carried to every tongue, tribe, and nation. Even those who are not summoned to go as missionaries are called to support missions with gifts and their prayers.

—*Larry Richards*

GOD CREATED ME TO HAVE A PERSONAL RELATIONSHIP WITH HIM

"In the beginning God created the heavens and the earth."

GENESIS 1:1

At first glance, Genesis 1:1 doesn't look like a promise. Grammatically it's a statement. And yet there are few verses in Scripture so rich in promissory intent. This first verse in the Bible introduces us to God, placing His work of creation in promise perspective.

The phrase "in the beginning" reminds us that matter is not eternal. There is more to this universe than fiery stars and stony planets whirling through space. This simple truth—that the universe had a beginning—opens the soul to look for life's meaning in origins. If matter existed eternally and life somehow derived from it, the universe would be cold and impersonal. Mute nature would be unaware and untouched by our birth or death, much less by our joys and sorrows.

The universe is not impersonal! Behind the material causes lies a Person—a being who is completely and fully aware. We human beings can relate to a Person! We are persons within a world whose origin is personal! The fact that the universe was designed by a Person holds out hope that we might possibly come to know Him. And, through a relationship with the Creator, we might discover meaning and purpose for our own lives!

The story of how God designed and shaped the universe fills us with hope. In the regularity of the seasons, we sense His faithfulness. In the stability of the heavens, we sense His trustworthiness. He whose power launched all that is intends to do us good!

Thus, the first verse in the Bible is full of promise, just as creation is. Both point us to the Creator. Both promise us that there is meaning to our existence. And both promise us that we can discover meaning for our lives in a personal relationship with God.

—Larry Richards

GOD KEEPS ME IN FELLOWSHIP WITH HIM THROUGH CHRIST

"If we walk in the light as He is in the light, we have fellowship with one another, and the blood of Jesus Christ His Son cleanses us from all sin."

1 JOHN 1:7

John frequently contrasted light and darkness in his writings. Some interpreters have suggested that "walking in the light" means to live without sin. But John had written that if we walk in the light Christ's blood cleanses us from sin. If those walking in the light need cleansing, walking in the light cannot mean living a sinless life.

The keys to understanding John's imagery are found in the phrase, "And do not practice the truth," and in what Scripture says about sin. In Scripture something is *true* because it is in harmony with reality. God's Word is truth (John 7:17), not simply because God said it, but because what God says reveals reality as He alone knows it.

The person walking in darkness is someone who is dishonest, neither facing nor admitting reality. He says he has fellowship with God, but he is not being honest about his life.

What does God say about the believer and sin? John reminded us that the truth is, "If we say that we have no sin, we deceive ourselves and the truth is not in us" (1 John 1:8). A person who walks in the light is honest with himself and God about his sins. He looks at himself as God views him, he acknowledges his flaws and faults, and he relies on the blood of Christ to keep on cleansing him. A person like this has fellowship with God.

God's promise is that if we are honest with ourselves and with Him about our sins, we will stay in fellowship with Him. How can a sinner have fellowship with a holy God? Only on the basis of the blood of Christ, which keeps on cleansing us from our sins.

—*Larry Richards*

God Gives Me His Personal Attention

"And you will be hated by all for My name's sake. But not a hair of your head shall be lost."

Luke 21:17, 18

Luke 21 contains special instructions that Jesus gave to His disciples shortly before His crucifixion. Together these constitute realistic warnings about dangers that lie ahead, along with encouragement to persevere. In 21:17–19, Jesus warned that the disciples would be hated for their commitment to Him. He urged them to be patient and persevere.

A saying of Jesus already reported in Luke 12:7 helps us understand the nature of this promise. In this verse, Christ told His followers that "the very hairs of your head are all numbered. Do not fear therefore; you are of more value than many sparrows."

Neither Luke 12:7 nor 21:8 teach that believers will be protected from all harm. What these verses do teach is that God gives His *personal attention* to His own. We are so important to the Lord that each hair of our head is numbered and precious in His sight.

We know from Scripture and from the thousands of
martyrs recorded in church history that Christians who
were committed to Jesus have been brutalized and
murdered. But from this and many other promises in
Scripture, we know that those martyrs were not aban-
doned by God. He was with them in their suffering,
and when death came He welcomed them into His
presence.

We may be uncertain about the future. But we can
never be uncertain about whether God is giving us His
personal attention. He is involved in the most minute
details of our lives.

—*Larry Richards*

GOD ACCEPTS ME AS ONE OF HIS CHILDREN

"Beloved, now we are the children of God; and it has not yet been revealed what we shall be, but we know that when He is revealed, we shall be like Him, for we shall see Him as He is."

1 JOHN 3:2

One of the major themes of God's New Covenant is inner transformation. Sinful human beings come into a relationship with God through which He changes them from within, to become more and more like Jesus. This inner transformation is a process that goes on throughout our lives.

The gospel of Jesus is for both *now* and *then*. Now, John reminds his readers, "we are the children of God." In Christ, a family relationship with God the Father has been established, and our status has been changed from enemies (cf. Rom. 5:10) to dearly loved children.

Knowing that we are children now does not tell us what we will become. We know that our destiny will be unveiled when Jesus comes. We know that we will be like Jesus. And we know that we will see Him as He is—in His full glory as God.

People tend to act in harmony with their self-image. A child who sees herself as stupid tends not to study or do well in school, even if she has the ability. An adult who sees himself as competent will seize opportunities for advancement at work that a person who thinks of himself as less competent would never attempt.

How does God want us to see ourselves? As His children now—and as children who are destined to be like Jesus. This is our essential identity: we are little Christs. And how will we act if we have the hope that we will be like Jesus one day? We will seek to purify ourselves even as Jesus is pure. We will seek to grow toward His perfect will for our lives.

—Larry Richards

GOD WORKS FOR MY GOOD

"We know that all things work together for good to those who love God, to those who are the called according to His purpose."

ROMANS 8:28

In Romans 8, Paul declared that lost and helpless sinners have been declared righteous by a loving God on the basis of Christ's death. Those who believe have not only been declared righteous; they have been given the Holy Spirit to enable them to actually be righteous by transforming them from within.

What can we say about our relationship with such a wonderful God of grace? One thing we can say with confidence is that "all things work together for good to those who love God." Paul does not ask us to believe that everything that happens to us *is* good. Some things that happen to us are terrible. Rather, Paul assures us that God is so great that He is able to work in any set of circumstances for our good. God's commitment to those who love Him is to work in and through every circumstance to our benefit.

Romans 8:29 goes on to define that "benefit." God's intent is that we should be "conformed to the image of His son." To become more like Jesus is the ultimate good. And God is able to work through all experiences we may have to make us more like our Lord.

This is a promise to which we are expected to respond. If we slip into despair when trials come, if we doubt God's love, or if we become angry, we are far less likely to experience the good that God intends. On the other hand, if we face our trials in the calm confidence that we are surrounded by the love of God, and if we ask God to teach us what He intends us to learn, we will experience His transforming touch.

—*Larry Richards*

GOD CLEANSES ME FROM SIN

"Though your sins are like scarlet, they shall be as white as snow; though they are red like crimson, they shall be as wool."

ISAIAH 1:18

The prophet Isaiah's first sermon is an indictment of God's people as evildoers. Yet God calls His people back to Him and promises that they can be cleansed. The reference to scarlet and crimson is significant. Many of the ancient dyes quickly faded. But crimson/scarlet dyes were the most permanent known in the ancient world. What a stunning promise—that God is able to make the permanently stained "white as snow!"

Isaiah framed this promise within the context of Moses' covenant (Is. 1:15–17, 19, 20). Yet promise of forgiveness and cleansing from sin is extended throughout Scripture to all people on the basis of faith. Anyone who wishes to establish a relationship with the Lord must come to Him as one stained with sin, yet with faith in God's promise of forgiveness.

This promise is not just a call to saving faith. It is a call to straying believers to repent and return to God's ways. However great our sins, God will cleanse us when we turn back to Him.

Some have assumed that a blanket promise of restoration is a license to sin. But love begets love. Sensing God's forgiving love, we have more motivation to want to please Him.

As for those who have sinned, the certain knowledge that our heavenly Father will welcome us when we return to Him is strong motivation for repentance and change. If sinning believers had only God's anger to look forward to, they might keep on running from Him. Knowing that we will be welcomed and forgiven encourages us to come home.

So the promise of cleansing is for every believer. As the promise draws the sinner back to God, its expression of God's unending love keeps the faithful near to Him.

—*Larry Richards*

GOD SAVES ME FROM HIS WRATH

"Much more then, having now been justified by His blood, we shall be saved from wrath through Him."

ROMANS 5:9

In Romans 1:16–3:23, the apostle Paul showed that all human beings, Jews as well as Gentiles, are sinners who fall short of the glory of God. In Romans 3:24 through Romans 5:11, Paul teaches justification by faith. In view of Jesus' death for us on the cross, God has declared those who believe in Jesus innocent and has credited believers with Christ's own righteousness.

The death of Christ serves as the basis for the great gospel promise that Paul proclaims: "Having been justified by His blood, we shall be saved from wrath through Him."

Both the Old and New Testaments speak of God's wrath or anger. In the Old Testament, God's anger is closely associated with Israel's rejection of His covenant. In the New Testament, there is a distinctly different focus. God's wrath is reserved for those who refuse to respond to the gospel. These persons are viewed as objects of God's wrath (John 3:36; Rom. 1:18; Eph. 2:3).

Also, in the New Testament God's wrath is linked exclusively with final judgment. The New Testament places God's expression of His wrath with the future, describing a time at history's end when God will unleash His anger on those who have refused to respond to His love and grace (see Matt. 3:7; Rom. 9:22; 2 Thess. 1:6–10).

We who believe have been justified (declared innocent) on the basis of Christ's blood. We can therefore *know* that when God's wrath is unleashed against sinners, we will be spared. Since we have been judicially declared innocent by God Himself, His anger will not be directed against us.

How wonderful to know that the justified will know only the love and grace of Him who has saved us. We have been saved from God's wrath.

—*Larry Richards*

GOD PROVIDES ACCESS TO SALVATION THROUGH HIS SON

"I am the door. If anyone enters by Me, he will be saved, and will go in and out and find pasture."

JOHN 10:9

In John 10, Christ used the image of a shepherd and his sheep to communicate spiritual truths. This imagery is rooted in the Old Testament, and not only in Psalm 23. Both Jeremiah and Ezekiel used the shepherd as a metaphor for spiritual leadership. Both prophets pictured Israel's leaders, charged by God with watching out for His people, as flawed and selfish. The prophets then looked forward to a time when God Himself would shepherd His people.

Through Ezekiel God promised, "I will establish one shepherd over them, and he shall feed them—My servant David. He shall feed them and be their shepherd" (Ezek. 34:23). In presenting Himself as Shepherd, Jesus again claimed to be the promised Messiah.

The sheepfold of biblical times was a corral made of rocks or thorns. It had only one opening. At night the shepherd led his sheep into this enclosure, and then he himself lay down across the opening as its "door." No thief or wild animal could harm the sheep without passing their protector.

In Jesus' teaching, "anyone who enters" through Christ becomes one of His sheep. Such a person is not only saved, but throughout life he or she will be shepherded by Jesus and led in and out to find pasture.

In this brief parable, Jesus presented Himself as the one through whom we gain access to salvation and the world to come. In the context of Christ's reference to Himself as the true Shepherd, Jesus called for His hearers to recognize Him as the promised Messiah of the Old Testament.

This promise of Jesus remains open to people today. Jesus is still the door of the sheep. And all people are invited to enter.

—*Larry Richards*

GOD FORGIVES ME

"For if you forgive men their trespasses, your heavenly Father will also forgive you. But if you do not forgive men their trespasses, neither will your Father forgive your trespasses."

—Matthew 6:14, 15

Several approaches have been taken to explain this difficult saying of Jesus.

The "you" is plural, and so the saying applies to the believing community. When forgiveness is not exercised in the local community, God will not overlook the community's flaws.

The "you" is "everyone," and the issue is eternal salvation. The person who forgives will be saved. This, of course, denies the clear teaching of the Bible that God forgives those who believe in Jesus on the basis of Christ's sacrificial death on Calvary (Acts 5:1; Rom. 4:7; Eph. 1:7).

The saying is addressed to believers individually, and is both a promise and a warning. God wants us to experience now the release that comes with assurance of forgiveness. But when our hearts are hard toward others and we refuse to forgive them, that release is denied to us as well.

Forgiveness is like a coin. To be genuine, a coin has both heads and tails. For forgiveness to be genuine, it must also have two dimensions—a receiving side and an extending side.

These verses are best taken as a commentary on that part of the Lord's Prayer which says, "And forgive us our debts [trespasses] as we forgive our debtors" (Matt. 6:12). Jesus does not make our forgiveness *dependent on* our willingness to forgive others. Rather, He forges a link in our thinking between forgiving others and experiencing forgiveness. No matter how we understand Jesus' saying, it is clear that a failure to be forgiving is harmful to our spiritual growth, while a willingness to extend forgiveness nurtures a deeper personal relationship with our forgiving Lord.

—*Larry Richards*

GOD PROVIDES
ATONEMENT FOR MY SINS

*"So the priest shall make atonement for his sin that he
has committed, and it shall be forgiven him."*

LEVITICUS 4:35

The law code that God gave to Israel defined sins and
condemned those who violated the laws. Leviticus
established a system of sacrifices through which sins
could be covered and the sinner could find forgiveness.
But the sacrifices established in the first seven chapters
of Leviticus were only for sins committed *unintentionally*
(cf. Lev. 4:2, 13, 22, 27; 5:15). But forgiveness was provided even for intentional sins. Once a year on the Day of
Atonement, the high priest made a prescribed sacrifice:
"For on that day the priest shall make atonement for
you, to cleanse you, that you may be clean from all your
sins before the Lord" (Lev. 16:30).

The sacrifices provided for God's Old Testament people teach many truths. They show that God is eager to
forgive sinning people. They teach that the punishment
of sin is death, but that God will accept the death of a
substitute. The sacrifices of the Old Testament foreshad-
owed Jesus' death on the cross and helped to define its

meaning. Jesus died as our substitute, paying the penalty for our transgression against God.

The promise of forgiveness acted out in the Old Testament is ours to claim today. The Book of Hebrews says of Christ's sacrifice:

We have been sanctified through the offering of the body of Jesus Christ once for all. And every priest stands ministering daily and offering repeatedly the same sacrifices, which can never take away sins. But this Man, after He had offered one sacrifice for sins forever, sat down at the right hand of God. . . . For by one offering He has perfected forever those who are being sanctified (Heb. 10:10–12, 14).

The forgiveness that is ours when we trust Christ as our sacrifice and Savior is perfect and complete.

—*Larry Richards*

GOD SAVES ME THROUGH A SACRIFICIAL DEATH

"Also for Adam and his wife the Lord God made tunics of skin, and clothed them."

GENESIS 3:21

Adam and Eve had sinned by disobeying God. The processes that lead to biological death were instituted, and spiritually Adam and Eve died the day they sinned. "And thus death spread to all men" (Rom. 5:12).

Without God's intervention, the destiny of Adam and Eve and all their descendants was fixed. But God still loved the first pair, so He chose to intervene. God clothed Adam and Eve with tunics of skin, symbolically covering their sins so they could continue to have a relationship with Him.

This was history's first sacrifice. The blood of a substitute was shed in order that the sin of human beings might be covered and a sinner might enter the presence of God. Here we have the promise of a redemption that God would make available to all humankind. Only by relying on the grace of God and by placing our faith in the promise that God will accept the death of a substitute in place of our own death can anyone be accepted by God.

This first promise of salvation tells us a great deal about God! It reveals His continuing love for human beings, His grace to us, and His power to save. The God who clothed Adam in skins is eager to clothe us as well, in that great exchange in which Jesus Christ takes our sins and gives us His righteousness. When we place our trust in Him, we are clothed indeed. We can claim the promise of redemption today only by coming to God through Jesus.

The promise of redemption is the one promise to which we *must* respond if we are to have a relationship with the Lord. Only by accepting Jesus as Savior, and thus placing our confidence in the blood He shed for us on Calvary, can we be redeemed.

—*Larry Richards*

God Declares Me Righteous on the Basis of Personal Faith

"Now to him who works, the wages are not counted as grace but as debt. But to him who does not work but believes on Him who justifies the ungodly, his faith is accounted for righteousness."

—Romans 4:4, 5

Those people who see law as a way of salvation assume that God's favor is something they can earn by what they do. Yet in Romans Paul argues that the real purpose of God's law is to serve as a mirror, reflecting mankind's sin and need of a Savior.

Paul was aware that the covenant promises were given to Abraham long before the birth of Isaac, while Abraham lived in Ur (Gen. 12:1–3, 7). Later when God promised the aged Abraham that a son from his own body would inherit the promise, Abraham believed God, and the Bible says that Abraham's *faith* [not his faithfulness!] was counted to him as righteousness (Gen. 15:6).

While the covenant promises were again confirmed
to Abraham after he displayed his loyalty to God in
the matter of preparing to sacrifice Isaac (Gen.
22:15–18), Abraham had been declared righteous years
before on the basis of his faith! The promise implicit in
God's relationship with Abraham was that God offers
salvation not "to him who works" but "to him who
does not work but believes on Him who justifies the
ungodly."

To the Jews of Paul's day, the salvation formula was
works = salvation as payment due. To the apostle Paul
and throughout the Scriptures, the true salvation formula was faith = salvation as a grace gift. This wonderful promise finds its source in the loving character
of our God, who has chosen to be gracious to the
ungodly, however little we deserve His favor.

As God declared Abraham righteous on the basis of
his faith, so today God will declare anyone righteous
who has an Abraham-like confidence in "Him who justifies the ungodly."

—*Larry Richards*

GOD DECLARES ME
BLAMELESS BEFORE CHRIST

[God] "will also confirm you to the end, that you may
be blameless in the day of our Lord Jesus Christ."

1 CORINTHIANS 1:8

This promise is woven into a long sentence expressing
Paul's thanks to God for the grace He has shown the
Corinthians (1 Cor. 1:4–8). Although the Corinthian
church was torn by dissension and far from blameless,
Paul remained confident about these Christians. His
confidence was certainly not based on their behavior.
Paul knew that God was able to accomplish His pur-
poses in the saved (see 2 Cor. 5:15, 16).

In the past God had confirmed Paul's testimony to
Christ by saving the Corinthians. In the future, when
Christ returns (1 Cor. 1:7), God's present guarantee of
salvation to believers would surely be confirmed. The
Corinthians would appear before Christ and be found
blameless (1 Cor. 1:8).

Paul's use of legal terminology as well as the reference to Jesus' return explains this promise. Paul made
no guarantee that the Corinthians would resolve all
their problems. He made no guarantee that they would

achieve godliness before Christ returned. But he did promise that God would treat the Corinthians as blameless—because of what Jesus had done for them.

The promise God made to the Corinthians is for all believers. We will also be counted blameless in "the day of our Lord Jesus Christ." This certainty moves true believers to want to live blamelessly in the present. The awesome love of God awakens love in our hearts and makes us want to please Him in all we do (see 2 Cor. 5:14).

—*Larry Richards*

GOD MAKES ME A NEW CREATION

"Therefore, if anyone is in Christ, he is a new creation; old things have passed away; behold, all things have become new."

2 CORINTHIANS 5:17

The apostle Paul explained to the Corinthian believers that the Holy Spirit was at work transforming believers into the image of Christ. What we see is always changing. But the unseen is eternal. One of the unseen realities on which the apostle counted is that if anyone is in Christ, he or she truly is a new creation.

The Corinthians appeared to give little evidence of Christ's transforming work in their lives. But a person who has trusted Jesus as Savior does have Christ in his heart. And Christ is there to work the transformation that He died to make possible.

For this reason, the apostle Paul no longer viewed the Corinthian believers from a human point of view, based on what could be observed in their lives. Instead, Paul looked to the unseen but eternal realities. He saw fellow believers as new creations in Christ. He was convinced that, by God's grace and in time, the immature and the unresponsive would respond to God's love, becoming the Christians they could be in Him.

The promise of the new creation is that "old things have passed away; behold, all things have become new" (2 Cor. 5:17). With Jesus in our lives, the grip of sin that once made us helpless has been broken. With Jesus in our lives, everything has become new. Life is filled with possibilities and rich with potential meaning.

When we trusted Jesus, the old was put behind us and everything did become new. Yet you and I, like the Corinthians, have a choice. We can go on living in the old way, moved by old passions and driven by the old values. Or we can open our lives to the Lord, letting Him give us new desires and engrave His values on our hearts.

—*Larry Richards*

GOD REFRESHES ME WITH LIVING WATER

"Whoever drinks of the water that I shall give him will never thirst. But the water that I shall give him will become in him a fountain of water springing up into everlasting life."

JOHN 4:14

Jesus was speaking to a Samaritan woman who had come to draw water from a well. Jesus had struck up a conversation by asking her for a drink. In the conversation, Jesus remarked that if she had known who He was, she would have asked Him for "living water."

In Judaism a distinction was made between water standing in a pool and "living" (running) water. Only running water could be used in the *mikvah*, or purifying bath used to make a Jew ritually clean after having become ritually unclean. It is possible that Jesus was drawing an analogy to this practice. If so, His teaching was that a person who accepts Christ has a purifying spring of water that flows from within.

The spring of water within satisfies a person's deepest spiritual needs. The implicit promise is that in giving us eternal life, Jesus provides us with a source of inner refreshment that meets our most basic needs.

Jesus' promise was made without conditions. The spring of inner refreshment exists within us. One commentator has written, "Christ satisfies a man not by banishing his thirst, which would be to stunt his soul's growth, but by bestowing upon him by the gift of His Spirit an inward source of satisfaction which perennially and spontaneously supplies each recurrent need of refreshment" (G. H. C. Macgregor).

Too often in times of pain or pressure we look everywhere for relief—except within, to Him, where Jesus' refreshing spring still bubbles up.

—*Larry Richards*

GOD FEEDS ME WITH THE BREAD OF LIFE

"I am the living bread which came down from heaven. If anyone eats of this bread, he will live forever; and the bread that I shall give is My flesh, which I shall give for the life of the world."

JOHN 6:51

Jesus had miraculously fed 5,000 people by multiplying a few loaves of bread. The miracle motivated the crowd to acclaim Jesus as king, not because they believed in Him but because He could feed them. They justified this action by pointing out that God had miraculously fed their forefathers with manna in the desert.

Jesus then preached what is called His "sermon on the bread of life." He presented Himself as the "true bread from heaven," which God has now miraculously provided to give and sustain spiritual life. Jesus reminded His listeners that their fathers ate manna in the desert—and died. In contrast, God has now provided a "bread" which "one may eat and never die." Jesus identified His flesh as the "bread" that He would give in order that those who "eat" might live forever.

Jesus was using the language of sacrifice. After offering up an animal, the offerer and his family ate part of the sacrificial animal. Through the sacrifice, the sinner had returned to God, and in the sacrifice God provided a meal that affirmed a protective relationship with Him. In His teaching, Jesus thus presented Himself as a sacrifice for humankind's sin, promising that those who symbolically partook of His sacrifice would be given everlasting life.

Saint Augustine summed up the meaning of "eating" Christ's flesh in three Latin words: *Crede, et manducasti*—"Believe, and you have eaten" (*Homilies on John,* 26:1). Through faith, men and women throughout the ages have participated in Christ's sacrifice. In return, they have been given God's gift of everlasting life. In the same way we may participate in Christ's sacrifice today.

—*Larry Richards*

GOD RESTORES ME TO HIS FELLOWSHIP

"He placed cherubim at the east of the garden of Eden, and a flaming sword which turned every way, to guard the way to the tree of life."

After Adam and Eve had sinned, God drove them from the Garden of Eden. Genesis explains that God's motive was to prevent them from taking the fruit of "the tree of life, and eat, and live forever" (Gen. 3:22).

The key to understanding this promise is in the placement of the cherubim and flaming sword to "guard" the way back to Eden. The cherubim and flaming sword were not placed there to keep human beings out of Eden, but *to keep the way home open*!

Here we see the promise of a restoration to innocence and perfect fellowship with God which Eden symbolizes. God will one day raise the saved to eternal life, and at that time will remove every taint of sin. Innocence will be restored and perfected. Once again, human beings will enjoy the most intimate relationship with the living God.

Until that day arrives, cherubim and a flaming sword guard the way to the tree of life. No hostile power can close the highway that Christ has opened through His death. In Christ, we can return to Eden and our fellowship with God is assured. By following the path stained by the sacrificial blood of Christ we can find our way back to our true home.

While we rejoice in the prospect of our return to Eden and a perfected innocence, the prospect creates a desire in us to live in holiness and purity. In the promise of restoration we see our true selves, as God created us to be. Drawn to that true self, we are motivated to live for God here and now.

—Larry Richards

GOD GIVES ME A NEW SELF

"He who finds his life will lose it, and he who loses his life for My sake will find it."

MATTHEW 10:39

Throughout Matthew 10, Jesus explained the dangers and rewards of discipleship. While in most cases the dangers are here on earth, the rewards are in the world to come. Yet this promise of Jesus points to a significant danger here and now as well as to a present reward.

The disciple's cross is not martyrdom, as some people in the early church assumed. Just as His cross was God's will for Jesus, so in Christian theology the cross can serve as a symbol of God's will for each believer. We are to meet each new day committed to doing God's will. In doing so, we take up our crosses and follow the example set by Jesus.

To understand the implications of this choice, we need to look at Matthew 16:25, 26, which expands the thought expressed in Matthew 10: "For whoever desires to save his life will lose it, but whoever loses his life for My sake will find it. For what profit is it to a man if he gains the whole world, and loses his own soul? Or what will a man give in exchange for his soul?"

The Greek word translated both "life" and "soul" is *psyche,* and it should be understood in the sense of "his very self." Jesus is telling us that the person who holds on to his old self—fearful of what it might cost to take up his cross and follow Jesus—loses the new "very own self" which he or she might become. Commitment to living as a disciple of Jesus is the secret to becoming all we can be!

—*Larry Richards*

God Continues to Transform My Life

"He who has begun a good work in you will complete it until the day of Jesus Christ."

Philippians 1:6

Paul began his letter with thanksgiving for the partnership of the Philippians in the gospel. He had established the church in their city, and he remained confident that God would continue to work in their lives.

The "good work" to which Paul referred was God's transforming work in salvation. This good work begins when we trust Christ as Savior; it continues throughout our lives as God the Holy Spirit gradually transforms us; it will be completed when Jesus comes and we are fully like Him at last.

In the Greek language, the word translated as "complete" means "to carry to completion." God will not abandon us or the work He set out to do in our lives when we came to Christ. He has a blueprint to follow: Christ's own perfect character. God is committed to complete our reconstruction in order to make us like Jesus.

Later in this letter Paul urged the Philippians to "work out your own salvation with fear and trembling"

(2:12). Doesn't this contradict the assurance message of Philippians 1:6? Not at all. Paul did not urge the Philippians to work *for* their salvation, nor was the "fear and trembling" a fear of possible rejection by God. Paul urged the Philippians to let the salvation that had changed them inside change their behavior, and thus be "worked out" in their daily lives. Even this "working out" of our salvation is not done on our own, for "it is God who works in you both to will and to do for His good pleasure" (Phil. 2:13).

All we need to fear is that by some failure to trust Him or some lack of commitment, the *process* of our transformation might be delayed.

—*Larry Richards*

GOD IS FAITHFUL IN SPITE OF MY UNFAITHFULNESS

"They are new every morning; great is Your faithfulness."

LAMENTATIONS 3:23

"Great is Your faithfulness," so great that there has never been an exception. Through the ages, our God has had billions of people to deal with. Yet there does not stand under heaven's cover, or above the stars, or in hell itself a single soul who can say that God is not absolutely faithful. No item in the list of our divine promises is unfulfilled. God remembers every promise that He ever made, and He honors each in the experience of those who believe in Him. They who trust in the Lord will find Him faithful, not only in great things, but also in little things. His faintest word will stand firm and steadfast. His least truth will never grow dim.

The glory of God's faithfulness is that no sin of ours has ever made Him unfaithful. Unbelief is a damning thing, yet even when we do not believe, God is faithful. His children might rebel. They might wander far from His statutes and be chastened with many stripes. Nevertheless, He says, "My lovingkindness I will not utterly take from him, nor allow My faithfulness to fail. My covenant I will not break, nor alter the word that has gone out of My lips" (Ps. 89:33, 34).

God's saints may fall under the cloud of His displeasure and provoke the Most High by their transgressions; still He will have compassion on them. He says, "I, even I, am He who blots out your transgressions for My own sake; and I will not remember your sins" (Is. 43:25). Thus, no sin of ours can make God unfaithful.

—*Charles Haddon Spurgeon*

GOD TAKES AWAY MY WORRY

"And which of you by worrying can add one cubit to his stature?"

LUKE 12:25

Christians are forbidden to be anxious (Matt. 6:31–34). "Look at the birds of the air," said Christ, "they neither sow nor reap nor gather into barns; yet your heavenly Father feeds them. Are you not more valuable than they?" (Matt. 6:26). If you have a Father in heaven who cares for you, every little bird that sits on a branch and sings, even though it doesn't have a grain of barley in all the world, should put you to shame if you are anxious.

Our Lord taught that anxiety is useless and needless. Care and worry cannot add one cubit to our stature (Luke 12:25). If the farmer worries about lack of rain, will this open the clouds of heaven? If the merchant is concerned because an unfavorable wind delays his loaded ship, can this turn the gale to another quarter? We do not improve our lot by fretting and fuming. If we were infinitely wiser we would throw our cares on God. Anxiety is folly, for it groans and worries and accomplishes nothing.

According to our Savior, anxiety about worldly things is heathenish, "For all these things the Gentiles seek" (Matt. 6:32). Heathens have no God, and so they try to be their own providence. The believer who can say, "God's providence is my inheritance," will not worry. Let the heirs of heaven live on a higher plane than sinners who live without God and without hope. If we cannot trust our great God, can we better direct our lives? If we are in Christ, let us believe in our God and leave the governing of both the outside world and the little world within to our heavenly Father.

—*Charles Haddon Spurgeon*

GOD CONSOLES ME IN MY GRIEF

"Father, I desire that they also whom You gave Me may be with Me where I am, that they may behold My glory which You have given Me; for You loved Me before the foundation of the world."

JOHN 17:24

We love God's people. They are exceedingly precious. Far too often we look on their deaths as a grievous loss. If we could confer immortality, we would never let them die. But it would be cruel to deprive them of a speedy entrance into their inheritance. We want to hold them here a little longer. We find it hard to relinquish our grasp, because the saint's departure causes us much pain. We are poorer because of the eternal enriching of the beloved, who have gone over to the majority and entered their rest.

Yet while we are sorrowing, Christ is rejoicing. In the advent of every one of His own to the skies, Jesus sees an answer to His prayer that they will be with Him (John 17:24). We are grieving, but He is rejoicing. Their deaths are painful in our sight, but "precious in the sight of the Lord is the death of His saints" (Ps. 116:15).

Tears are permitted, but they must glisten in the light of faith and hope. "Jesus wept" (John 11:35), but He never complained. We may weep, but not "as [those] who have no hope" (1 Thess. 4:13). There is great cause for joy in the departure of our loved ones.

It cannot be precious to God to see the highest works of His hand torn in pieces, to see His skillful embroidery in the human body broken, defiled, and given to decay. Yet to the believer, it is not death to die. It is a departure out of this world to the Father, an entrance into the Kingdom.

—*Charles Haddon Spurgeon*

GOD GIVES ME VICTORY OVER PAIN AND DEATH

"Look on my affliction and my pain, and forgive all my sins."

PSALM 25:18

I have suffered as much pain as most. I also know as much about depression as anyone. Still, my Master's service is a blessed service. Faith in Him makes my heart leap for joy. I would not change places with the healthiest, wealthiest, or most famous if I had to give up my faith in Jesus Christ.

I visited a beloved sister from my congregation. She was dying with consumption, and death was near. She could scarcely speak, but what she said was full of sacred joy. She is in heaven now, and heaven was in her then. "I am so much closer," said she, "to the better land. I have fewer of these hard breaths to fetch and fewer of these hard pains to bear. I shall soon be where Jesus is." She talked as freely about dying and going home as I talk about going to my house for dinner.

Before she died, she felt as if she was going through a river. She said that she was in the midst of it and that floods were around her. In an interval of consciousness, she said, "I am going up the other side. The waters are shallower. I am climbing the other bank. Jesus is coming for me! I can hear the music of heaven." Her heart seemed overpowered with some sweet mystic melody that reached her inner spirit.

Thank God, most do not suffer as much as this dear saint did. Yet there was never a person more calm, more comfortable, and more joyous on a deathbed than this daughter of affliction.

It does my soul good to see the Lord's people depart this life. I grieve that they are taken away to heaven, for we want them here. But I thank God for the evidences of His hope and love.

—Charles Haddon Spurgeon

GOD ANSWERS MY PRAYERS WHEN THEY REFLECT HIS WILL

"If you abide in Me, and My words abide in you, you will ask what you desire, and it shall be done for you."

JOHN 15:7

The word translated "abide" means to "remain in." In this verse, Jesus' words are His *rhemata*, His individual teachings, rather than His *logos*, His teaching in its entirety. To stay close to Jesus, we are not obligated to obey perfectly all that Christ has taught. If that were the case, only the most knowledgeable and mature believers could hope for their prayers to be answered!

No, Jesus placed His emphasis on our response to specific teachings. As we learn each new truth and respond to that truth with faith and obedience, we maintain a relationship with the Lord in which He is free and answers our prayers.

There is another truth in this verse that relates specifically to the prayer promise. As Jesus' words infuse us and shape our lives, His words will also shape our desires. We will increasingly want what Jesus wants. And, as Jesus' desires were in harmony with the will of God, so His prayers reflected God's will. When we desire what God wants and we make these desires a matter of prayer, we can be confident that "it shall be done for you."

Closeness to Jesus maintained by daily obedience to His *rhemata* is the key to fruitfulness. It is also a key to efficacious prayer. This is not because our obedience merits God's blessing. A more intimate relationship with Jesus will shape our thoughts and desires, bringing our prayers into harmony with God's will.

—*Larry Richards*

GOD CARES FOR ME LIKE A TENDER SHEPHERD

"I am the good shepherd; and I know My sheep, and am known by My own."

JOHN 10:14

God has not left us. He has not left us as the ostrich leaves her eggs on the ground to be crushed by a foot (Job 39:13–15). God is watching over us every moment. He exercises an unceasing care and a watchful providence; therefore, we should praise Him.

Some people think of God as having taken the universe like a watch, wound it, and placed it under His pillow and gone to sleep. This is not true. God's finger is on every wheel of the world's machinery. God's power is the force in the laws of the universe.

Child of Adam, you are not rocked in your cradle by wild winds but by the hand of love. Daughter of affliction, you are not bedridden to be the victim of heartless laws. There is One who, with His own kind and tender hand, makes your bed in sickness.

Day by day God gives us our daily bread and clothes us. He gives breath for our heaving lungs and blood for our beating hearts. He keeps us alive. If His

power were withdrawn we would immediately sink
into death.

"I am the good shepherd; and I know My sheep"
(John 10:14). You are the sheep of His hand. The hourly
provision, the constant protection, the wise and judi-
cious governing, the royal leadership through the
desert to the pastures on the other side of Jordan, the
power to chase away the wolf, and the skills to find
pasture in the wilderness—all these flow from the fact
that He is your Shepherd.

Praise Him! Adore the God who keeps you living
and feeds you from the storehouse of divine grace. Serve
Him with all your heart, soul, and strength. "You are His
people and the sheep of His pasture" (Ps. 100:3).

—*Charles Haddon Spurgeon*

GOD ASSURES ME THAT I WILL NEVER BE SEPARATED FROM HIS LOVE

"For I am persuaded that neither death nor life, nor angels nor principalities nor powers, nor things present nor things to come, nor height nor depth, nor any other created thing, shall be able to separate us from the love of God which is in Christ Jesus our Lord."

ROMANS 8:38, 39

The apostle Paul makes it clear in the Book of Romans that God is for us (Rom. 8:31). We have been acquitted by God Himself; no one can now bring any charge against us (Rom. 8:33). Nothing in this universe can separate us from the love of God in Christ Jesus our Lord.

This promise is clear and its intent is unmistakable. The believer who has put his or her trust in Jesus is safe in God's love. Earlier in Romans, Paul pointed out while we were yet sinners, Christ died for us (Rom. 5:6–8). Just as surely, "When we were enemies we were reconciled to God through the death of His Son, much more, having been reconciled, we shall be saved by His life" (Rom. 8:10). If God loved us so much while we were "yet sinners," how much more must He love us now!

This passage points to two realities which should give us confidence that believers will never be separated from God's love.

First, Christ died for us when we were sinners. On the basis of Jesus' death, God has declared us innocent and credited Christ's righteousness to our account. How could we imagine that such a God would turn against us?

Second, it is unimaginable that Christ should have sacrificed Himself for nothing. He shed His blood to save us. Because of Calvary, we have been forgiven and Jesus' righteousness has been credited to our account. If a person who has been saved by Christ's blood could later be lost, Jesus' death would have been ineffective. And this is unimaginable.

—*Larry Richards*

GOD WILL KEEP ME SAFE IN THE SAVIOR'S HANDS

"My Father, who has given them to Me, is greater than all; and no one is able to snatch them out of My Father's hand."

JOHN 10:29

Our position is guaranteed, and it is a place of honor, for we are in Christ's hands (John 10:28). It is a place of property, for Christ holds His people, and all the saints are in His hand. It is a place of love: "See, I have inscribed you on the palms of My hands, your walls are continually before Me" (Is. 49:16). It is a place of guidance (Ps. 32:8) and protection (Ps. 59:16).

No one will snatch us out of God's hands (John 10:28). As arrows are to be used by a mighty warrior, as jewels are to be used by a bride, so are we in the hand of Christ, for we are the ring on His finger.

John 10:28 reminds us that there are some who want to snatch us out of our Savior's hand. Some will rise and show great signs and wonders to deceive even the elect (Matt. 24:24). Roaring persecutors want to frighten God's saints and make them turn back. Scheming tempters desire to drag us to destruction.

Even our own heart tries to snatch us from His hand. But Jesus says, "Neither shall anyone snatch them out of My hand."

"Neither death nor life, nor angels nor principalities nor powers, nor things present nor things to come, nor height nor depth, nor any other created thing, shall be able to separate us from the love of God which is in Christ Jesus our Lord" (Rom. 8:38, 39). No person, devil, or conceivable thing is able to snatch us from His hand. Under no circumstances can anyone, by any scheme, remove us from being His favorites, His property, and His protected children.

—*Charles Haddon Spurgeon*

GOD WILL NOT FORSAKE ME

"Do not forsake me, O Lord; O my God, be not far from me!"

PSALM 38:21

We frequently pray that God will not forsake us in our hours of trials and tests. But we need to use this prayer all the time. There is not a moment in our lives that we can do without His constant upholding. Whether in light or in darkness, in fellowship or in temptation, we need to pray, "Do not forsake me, O Lord." "Hold me up and I shall be safe" (Ps. 119:117). A little child learning to walk needs the hand of her mother. The ship without a captain drifts from its course. We cannot make it without continued aid from above.

Pray, "Do not forsake me, O Lord." Father, do not forsake Your child, or I will fall by the hand of the enemy. Shepherd, do not forsake Your lamb, or I will wander from the safety of the fold. Great Vineyard Keeper, do not leave your plant, or I will wither and die. "Do not forsake me, O Lord," now or at any moment of my life.

Do not forsake me in my joys, lest they fully engage my heart. Do not forsake me in my sorrow, lest I murmur against You. Do not forsake me during repentance, lest I lose the hope of pardon and fall into despair.

Do not forsake me. Without You I am weak; with You I am strong. Do not forsake me. My path is dangerous and full of snares. I desperately need Your guidance.

The hen does not forsake her chickens. Cover me with Your feathers, and under Your wings I will take refuge (Ps. 91:4). "Be not far from me. Trouble is near and there is none to help" (Ps. 22:11). "Do not leave me nor forsake me, O God of my salvation" (Ps. 27:9).

—*Charles Haddon Spurgeon*

GOD GIVES ME HOPE FOR THE FUTURE

"Do not boast about tomorrow, for you do not know what a day may bring forth."

PROVERBS 27:1

A Christian can look forward to tomorrow with joy. Tomorrow is a happy thing. It is one stage nearer glory, one step nearer heaven, one more mile sailed across life's dangerous sea, one mile closer to home.

Tomorrow is a fresh lamp of the fulfilled promise that God has placed in His firmament. Use it as a guiding star or as a light to cheer your path. Tomorrow the Christian may rejoice. You may say that today is black, but I say that tomorrow is coming. You will mount on its wings and flee. You will leave sorrow behind.

Look forward to tomorrow with ecstasy, because our Lord may come. Tomorrow, Christ may be on this earth. "Therefore you also be ready, for the Son of Man is coming at an hour you do not expect" (Matt. 24:44). Tomorrow, we may all be in heaven. Tomorrow, we may lean on Christ's breast.

Tomorrow, or perhaps before then, this head will wear the crown (James 1:12). This arm will wave the

palm (Rev. 7:9). This lip will sing the song (Rev. 5:13).
This foot will walk the golden streets (Rev. 21:18).
Tomorrow, this heart will be full of immortal, everlasting, eternal bliss (Rev. 21:4). Be of good cheer, fellow
Christian, tomorrow can have nothing negative for
you.

"Do not boast about tomorrow, for you do not
know what a day may bring forth" (Prov. 27:1); rather,
comfort yourself with tomorrow. You have a right to
do that. You cannot have a bad tomorrow. It may be
the best day of your life, for it may be your last day on
earth.

—*Charles Haddon Spurgeon*

GOD PROMISES ME A BETTER LIFE BEYOND THE GRAVE

"For lo, the winter is past, the rain is over and gone."

SONG OF SOLOMON 2:11

The time is approaching when we will lie on our deathbeds. Oh long-expected day, come quickly! The best thing a Christian can do is die and be with Christ, for this is "far better" (Phil. 1:23) than life in the flesh. When we lie on our deathbeds panting out our lives, we shall remember that the winter is forever past. No more of this world's trials and troubles are ours, for "the rain is over and gone" (Song 2:11). No more stormy doubts, no more dark days of affliction.

We have come to the land Beulah (Is. 62:4). We sit on beds of spices. We can almost see the celestial city on the hilltop, just the other side of death's narrow stream. "The time of singing has come" (Song 2:12). Angelic songs are heard in the sickroom. The heart sings, and midnight melodies cheer the quiet entrance of the grave. "Though I walk through the valley of the shadow of death, I will fear no evil" (Ps. 23:4). These words are sweet birds that sing in the groves by the side of the river Jordan.

The voice of the turtledove is heard in the land (Song 2:12). Calm, peaceful, and quiet, the soul rests in the consciousness that there is now no condemnation to those who are in Christ Jesus (Rom. 8:1). "The fig tree puts forth her green figs, and the vines with the tender grapes give a good smell" (Song 2:13).

You who are believers in Christ, look forward to death with great joy. Expect it as your springtime of life, the time when your real summer will come and your winter will be over forever.

—*Charles Haddon Spurgeon*

GOD ASSURES ME THAT JESUS WILL COME AGAIN

"So Christ was offered once to bear the sins of many.
To those who eagerly wait for Him He will appear a
second time, apart from sin, for salvation."

HEBREWS 9:28

First-century Judaism looked forward to the coming of a royal Messiah who would save the nation from foreign oppressors and establish a powerful earthly kingdom. But Jesus, although He was the Messiah, had not met these expectations. This must have concerned the Jewish Christians to whom the Book of Hebrews was addressed.

The writer noted that "Christ was offered once" to bear the sins of many. The name *Christ* is the Greek translation of the Hebrew name for the promised Old Testament Messiah. The Messiah had come. And His first ministry was to be offered up as a sacrifice, that He might bear the sins of many.

But there was more to the Messiah's story. Christ was destined to appear "a second time." And when Jesus the Messiah returned, according to the writer of Hebrews, there would be a very different agenda.

The mission of Jesus in His first coming was to deal with sin. He died on the cross and paid the penalty of sin for all humankind. But the mission of Jesus in His second coming would be "for salvation." God's Old Testament "plan of [earthly] salvation for Israel" was that the Messiah would deal with Israel's enemies and establish an earthly kingdom. The writer of Hebrews assured his Jewish readers that the prophets' hopes and expectations would still be fulfilled. God remained faithful to His ancient covenant promises.

Sometimes Christians see only the New Testament promises concerning personal salvation and overlook other aspects of God's plan. One day the Christ who has redeemed us by His blood will return, to establish His rule over all the earth.

—*Larry Richards*

GOD WILL REUNITE ME WITH MY LOVED ONES

"For the Lord Himself will descend from heaven with a shout, with the voice of an archangel, and with the trumpet of God. And the dead in Christ will rise first. Then we who are alive and remain shall be caught up together with them in the clouds to meet the Lord in the air. And thus we shall always be with the Lord."

1 THESSALONIANS 4:16, 17

During the brief time that Paul was in Thessalonica, he taught many basic Christian doctrines. One doctrine was that of the *parousia*, the second coming of Jesus Christ. The prospect excited the Thessalonians, and they looked forward eagerly to Christ's return.

But as time went on, some in the church died. Their loved ones were troubled. What would happen to the dead when Jesus returned? Had those who died missed out on the blessings associated with Jesus' return?

In 1 Thessalonians 4:13–18, Paul dealt with this concern and conveyed one of Scripture's most wonderful promises. He first reaffirmed his teaching about the Second Coming. "The Lord Himself will descend from heaven with a shout, with the voice of an archangel, and with the trumpet of God." Then Paul went on to describe what Jesus' return would mean for believers who had died, and for those who were still alive at His coming.

Christians who have died will be raised and given resurrection bodies. Living Christians will be transformed at the same moment and given their resurrection bodies (cf. 1 Cor. 15:51). And loved ones who have died will be reunited with the living. We will all be caught up *together*. Christ's return will mean not only transformation but reunion with our loved ones as well.

We grieve when our loved ones in the Lord die. But we never despair. We have God's promise of reunion when Jesus returns.

—*Larry Richards*

GOD GIVES ME
IMPORTANT WORK TO DO
IN HIS KINGDOM

"Follow Me, and I will make you become fishers of men."

MARK 1:17

This call and promise was addressed to fishermen whom Jesus had chosen as His disciples. In first-century Judaism, "disciples" lived and traveled with a rabbi to master his teachings and copy his lifestyle. Becoming a disciple meant making a significant commitment.

Fishing was an occupation that helped meet the need of Palestine's population for protein. But fishers of men were called to meet the deepest need of every human being—the need of a personal relationship with God. Jesus' call of these fishermen to discipleship thus connected making the significant choice of discipleship with a significant future. The disciples chose the future that Jesus held out to them, and "immediately left their nets and followed him" (Mark 1:18).

Jesus' promise was made to several first-century fishermen by the Sea of Galilee. They met the one condition that they choose to follow Jesus. And history makes it clear that Jesus kept His promise. These ordinary men did become fishers of men, and indeed launched the church that Jesus founded with His blood. In following Jesus, they truly became significant people.

The promise was given to the first disciples, not to us. But throughout history those who have chosen to follow Jesus have been used by God to touch others with the good news of His Son, and thus have become significant indeed.

We can make the choice of those first disciples. And we can be sure that if we do, our lives will also become significant. There is nothing more important than witnessing for Jesus Christ and bringing others into His kingdom.

—*Larry Richards*

GOD BLESSES ME WITH GIFTS TO BE USED FOR HIM

"The manifestation of the Spirit is given to each one for the profit of all."

1 CORINTHIANS 12:7

The Corinthians were overly impressed by the more obvious and noticeable gifts of the Holy Spirit. They assumed that people who possessed such gifts as speaking in tongues were more spiritual than those with more ordinary gifts. Paul took up this issue in 1 Corinthians 12–14.

Paul introduced this section by saying, "Now concerning spiritual *gifts*" (1 Cor. 12:1). The word *gifts* is not in the Greek text, and the verse should be rendered "now concerning *spirituality*." In these chapters, Paul showed the relationship of the gifts of the Spirit to spirituality (ch. 12), identified the marks of true spirituality (ch. 13), and showed how spiritual gifts are to be used in the church (ch. 14).

"The manifestation of the Spirit is given to each one" is a stunning gospel promise. God the Holy Spirit expresses His presence in the life of each believer through one or more gifts. Spiritual gifts are evidence of the presence of the Holy Spirit in the lives of believers. There are many different gifts, some supernatural, some natural and ordinary. Yet each gift is an expression of the Holy Spirit's work.

Spiritual gifts are not given so Christians can identify the "spiritual" among them. Spiritual gifts are given to benefit the entire body of Christ. As each person exercises his or her gift, others are encouraged and built up in the faith.

While the promise as stated was part of Paul's teaching intended to correct the Corinthians' misunderstanding of spirituality, it is a wonderful promise for us. God has given each of us His Spirit, and the Holy Spirit *will* manifest His presence through some gift that he has given us. As the Spirit expresses Himself through each of us, others in Christ's body will grow in the faith.

—*Larry Richards*

GOD WILL GIVE ME THE STRENGTH TO DO HIS WORK

"I will certainly be with you."

EXODUS 3:12

When God called Moses to return to Egypt, Moses emphasized his lack of ability. He was not being humble. He had lost all confidence in himself. In his own eyes, Moses was a failure. When the door of opportunity suddenly opened, he was unwilling to enter.

The promise "I will be with you" is repeated to different people a dozen times in the Old Testament. It is one of the most basic of the commitments that God makes to individuals. The same promise is expressed in many ways. For instance, several times in the Old Testament God stated, "I will never leave you or forsake you" (Deut. 31:6, 8; Josh. 1:5; 1 Chron. 28:20). Thus, while this promise was made specifically to Moses, it is a promise that we can claim as well.

In Moses' confrontation with the leader of his world's greatest power, God would always be at his side. God did not expect Moses to do God's work on his own. He would undergird His servant with His personal presence as Moses confronted the pharaoh of Egypt.

The fact that the promise of God's presence is found so frequently in the Scripture underlines its importance. This is a promise God wants us never to forget. When God calls us to a task, He never leaves it to us alone. God stays with us so the power we need to accomplish His purpose is always available.

Moses felt overwhelmed by the task to which God was calling him. We can understand his reaction. How often have we hesitated, wondering "who am I?" But like Moses, we ask the wrong question. The question we should ask is, "Who is *God*?" If we answer that He is the all-powerful, we will hesitate no longer. The all-powerful will be with us, so we can face our challenges with confidence.

—Larry Richards

GOD ASSURES MY SUCCESS IN DOING KINGDOM WORK

"Then they will heed your voice."

EXODUS 3:18

When he was called to deliver God's people from slavery, Moses' first challenge was to win acceptance by the leaders of his own people. He wondered if he would seem to be a simple old man from the desert with a wild tale of being called by God to free the Israelites.

When we undertake any task, the outcome is uncertain. We never know if we will find success or failure. But God left no room for doubt when He encouraged Moses to go to Egypt. As for the leaders of His people, "They will heed your voice" (Ex. 3:18). Success was assured.

God also told Moses that success with the pharaoh would not be *easy*. The king of Egypt would refuse to release his slaves. But even this warning was accompanied by the promise of ultimate success. "I will stretch out My hand and strike Egypt . . . after that he will let you go" (Ex. 3:20). God's presence was a guarantee of

God's involvement in Moses' mission! And this assured success.

We are reminded that where God is present He is also involved. In one sense, this reality is a blanket promise of success given to every Christian.

It is important that our own measure of "success" be that used by the Lord. The prophet Isaiah reminds us, "So shall My word be that goes forth from My mouth; it shall not return to Me void; but it shall accomplish what I please, and it shall prosper in the thing for which I sent it" (Is. 55:11).

Whatever task God sets before us, He will be involved. Whatever we do for Him is sure to succeed. As Paul reminds us, "Therefore, my beloved brethren, be steadfast, immovable, always abounding in the work of the Lord, knowing that your labor is not in vain in the Lord" (1 Cor. 15:58).

—*Larry Richards*

GOD MAKES ME PRODUCTIVE IN HIS SERVICE

"I am the vine, you are the branches. He who abides in Me, and I in him, bears much fruit; for without Me you can do nothing."

JOHN 15:5

The image of God's people as a vine goes back to the Old Testament. Isaiah 5 records a complaint that God lodged against Israel. The Lord had carefully planted and tended His vine, Israel, in a vineyard. The Lord had a right to expect from Israel the good fruit of justice and righteousness. But instead Israel produced the sour grapes of injustice and sin.

Jesus expects a fruitful life of believers. His promise to those who abide in Him lays the foundation for our understanding of fruitful Christian living. No branch which has been separated from its vine can produce fruit. The vine is the source of vitality; nourishment required to produce fruit flows through the vine to its branches. By analogy, believers must live in close connection with Jesus if they are to have fruitful lives.

Jesus is the source of the spiritual nourishment we require to produce the fruit of love, joy, peace, and godliness.

Jesus explained how believers can "abide in" (stay connected to) Him. We maintain an intimate relationship with Jesus when we keep His commandments (John 15:10), and especially when we live by the commandment to love one another as Jesus has loved us (John 15:12). While God has chosen us and appointed us to produce fruit (John 15:16), whether we produce fruit depends on our daily decision to remain obedient to Him.

As we make the choice of obedience to Jesus each day, we can count on Him to keep His promise. Jesus will work in our hearts, and His power will produce the fruit that God longs to see.

—*Larry Richards*

GOD USES MY WEAKNESS FOR HIS GLORY

"My grace is sufficient for you, for My strength is made perfect in weakness."

2 CORINTHIANS 12:9

Paul turned to God for relief from his "thorn in the flesh" (2 Cor. 12:7). In spite of his repeated prayers, God turned down his request. Instead the Lord gave Paul the promise quoted in 1 Corinthians 12:9.

Rather than remove Paul's thorn, God promised the apostle His grace. God also stated a basic spiritual principle. His strength is made perfect in our weakness. Our weakness clears the way for God's strength to be given its fullest expression. Paul not only accepted God's "no"; he even rejoiced in it. Paul would take pleasure in weaknesses of every sort, since when he was weak he was actually strong!

The paradoxical principle expressed in God's promise to Paul undergirds all ministry. When we see ourselves as strong, we tend to rely on ourselves rather than the Lord. God alone is able to work miracles in the hearts of human beings. When we see ourselves as weak, we rely on Him. Thus our weakness opens channels in our lives through which God's power can flow.

There is another reason why our weaknesses enable God to express His strength. When others see us as strong, they tend to credit us with what God accomplishes through us. Paul was not ashamed that his Corinthians critics viewed him as weak. If they did, it had to be clear even to them that whatever Paul did was due to God's work through him. Thus God was given the glory due Him, and Paul's position as a servant of God was authenticated.

When we understand the paradox, we are freed from fear of our own inadequacy. Awareness of our weakness should encourage us to step out in faith. In our weakness we will rely on the Lord. And as we rely on Him, God's strength will be displayed in us.

—*Larry Richards*

GOD BLESSES OTHERS THROUGH MY TRIALS

"And at the ninth hour Jesus cried out with a loud voice, saying, 'Eloi, Eloi, lama sabachthani?' which is translated, 'My God, My God, why have You forsaken Me?'"

MARK 15:34

Some of you are called to suffer in your minds, not because of any wrong but for the sake of others. Some years ago, I preached a sermon from the text, "My God, My God, why have You forsaken Me?" (Mark 15:34). I preached my own cry. I felt an agony of spirit. I was under an awful sense of being forsaken by God, and I could not understand why I was surrounded by such thick darkness. I wanted to clear myself if any sin remained in me, but I could not discover any evil that I was tolerating.

When I went back into the vestry, I learned the secret of my personal distress. There was an elderly man in a horror of great darkness. He said, "I have never met any person who has been where I am. I trust there is hope." I asked him to sit down, and we talked. I hope I conducted him from the verge of insanity to the open healthy place of peace through believing. I could never have helped if I had not been in the miry clay myself. Then I understood why I felt like one forsaken. The Lord was leading me to where I would be taught to know this man, to where I would be willing to sit with him in the dark prison-house and lend him a hand to escape.

You must have faith in God and be sure that your trials will have great compensation. Be satisfied to endure hardness with the full belief that it is all right and that God will not only bring you through, but also bless somebody through your trials.

—Charles Haddon Spurgeon

GOD GUARANTEES MY CONTINUING USEFULNESS IN HIS SERVICE

"Now Moses was tending the flock of Jethro his father-in-law, the priest of Midian. And he led the flock to the back of the desert, and came to Horeb, the mountain of God."

EXODUS 3:1

Some of God's best workers have been laid aside for long periods. Moses was forty years in the desert, doing nothing but tending sheep. When you are retired or inactive, prepare for the time when God will again use you. If you are put on the shelf, do not rust; pray that the Master will polish you, so that when He uses you again you will be fully ready for the work.

While you are laid aside, I want you to pray for others who are working. Help them and encourage them. Do not get into that peevish, miserable frame of mind that resents and undervalues other's efforts. When they cannot do anything, some people do not like anybody else to work. Promise that if you cannot

help, you will never hinder. Spend time in prayer so
you may be fit for the Master's use.

At the siege of Gibraltar, the governor fired red-hot
shot down on the men-of-war. The enemy did not care
for the governor's warm reception. Think how it was
done. Here were gunners on the ramparts firing away,
and every garrison soldier wanted to join them. What
did those who could not fire a gun do? They heated
the shot. And that is what you must do.

Your pastor is the master gunner, so heat the shot
for him. Keep the furnace going, so that when a sermon is fired off it will be red-hot because of your
earnest prayers. When you see your friends sitting in
Sunday school or standing in the street working for
God, if you cannot join them, say, "Never mind. If I
can contribute nothing else, my prayers will heat the
shot."

—Charles Haddon Spurgeon

GOD WILL REWARD ME FOR WORK DONE FOR HIM

"Therefore, my beloved brethren, be steadfast, immovable, always abounding in the work of the Lord, knowing that your labor is not in vain in the Lord."

1 CORINTHIANS 15:58

One day death will be swallowed up in Christ's victory, and all His own will "put on immortality." This promise is found in the final phrase of 1 Corinthians 15:58: "Your labor is not in vain in the Lord."

A person can win a vast fortune, only to leave it all at death. A person can develop his or her talents and gain fame. Yet few of our earthly accomplishments will be remembered. But what we do to serve and glorify God is never meaningless. It echoes on throughout eternity.

When believers are raised at history's end, we will see the results of our labor for the Lord reflected in those around us. And God will not forget our labor of love. Second Corinthians 5:10 reminds us that "we must all appear before the judgment seat of Christ, that each one may receive the things done in the body, according to what he has done, whether good or bad."

The "judgment seat" was the *bema*—a raised platform in hellenistic cities from which public proclamations were made. While evil deeds were denounced from the *bema,* honors and praise were also proclaimed for the whole city to hear.

Honors and praise for believers are referred to in 1 Corinthians 15:58. In the day of Christ, all that we have done for Him will be acknowledged. In the words of the apostle Paul, "then each one's praise will come from God" (1 Cor. 4:5).

The only rewards with lasting value are those given by the Lord. This realization leads us to set new priorities. If we look ahead eagerly to resurrection and to eternity, we will commit ourselves joyfully to labor for the Lord.

—*Larry Richards*

God's Promises

GOD IS ALWAYS WITH ME

"Behold, I am with you and will keep you wherever you go, and will bring you back to this land; for I will not leave you until I have done what I have spoken to you."

GENESIS 28:15

During his flight to his mother's relatives, Jacob had a vision of God and of angels passing between heaven and earth. God announced that the covenant promises given to Abraham would pass to Jacob and his descendants. With this restatement of the covenant promises, God gave Jacob this personal promise.

God would keep Jacob *wherever* he might go, and would bring him safely back to Canaan. And God would not leave Jacob before all His promises to him were fulfilled. This promise is rooted in the nature of our everywhere-present God and in God's unshakable commitment to His people.

The promise revealed an aspect of God which underlines the differences between Him and pagan gods. The peoples of the ancient world identified their gods with the territory that the gods were supposed to "own." It was common practice for a traveler to show respect for the gods of the lands through which he passed, since those gods were thought to influence events within their territories.

While this promise was given to Jacob, it surely applies to us as well. The God who is everywhere is with us as He was with Jacob. God will not leave us until He has done all He has promised us in Christ.

The promise of God's presence involves both space and time. Wherever we may travel, our God is by our side. And whatever the future holds for us, God will be there. We can place our hand in His with confidence, finding peace in the certainty that His presence goes with us.

—Larry Richards

GOD IS THERE WHEN THINGS GO WRONG

"The Lord will fight for you, and you shall hold your peace."

EXODUS 14:14

The Israelites left Egypt and set out toward the Sinai wilderness. The cloudy-fiery pillar led them into what seemed to be a trap. The people's way was blocked on three sides and a pursuing Egyptian army closed in.

God Himself had led His people into this impossible situation. God was about to impress upon His people that their safety did not depend on them but on Him. Israel was told to "stand still." God would fight "and you shall hold your peace."

This promise was specific to its time and place. God does not generally expect us to do nothing. In contrast, God called on the Israelites when they invaded Canaan to be courageous in battle (cf. Josh. 1:5, 9). We can hardly generalize from this promise to our difficult situations today. But there are two significant lessons for us in this story.

First, God may lead us into difficult situations. It's natural to expect everything to turn out well if we have made a choice that we believe is God's will. It's also natural to wonder when that choice turns out badly. Did we misinterpreted God's will? The Israelites' experience reminds us that God does not always lead His people in pleasant pathways. He may lead us into situations that challenge our faith.

Second, God has His own purposes in choosing a path for us. In the case of Israel at the Red Sea, His purpose was to show Israel more of His power and to increase their faith. We often grow more spiritually during a week of stress than an entire year of ease.

Let's follow God's will as best we can, without second-guessing if things should go wrong. When we do what is right and troubles follow, we can look with confidence to the Lord, certain that He has a purpose in the experience.

—*Larry Richards*

GOD IS INVOLVED IN MY DAILY STRUGGLES

"No man shall be able to stand before you all the days
of your life; as I was with Moses, so I will be with
you. I will not leave you nor forsake you."

JOSHUA 1:5

This verse in Joshua promises God's active aid, for this
is the meaning of the phrase, "I will be with you." The
basic promise is repeated five times—at the beginning,
during, and following the conquest of Canaan (see
Josh. 1:9; 10:8; 11:16; 23:10). The promises encouraged
Joshua and the Israelites as they struggled to occupy
Canaan.

As Israel then lived under Moses' Law, the promise
of aid was conditional. An incident highlights this fact.
A man named Achan took spoils of war from Jericho
after the Lord had specifically commanded the people
not to do so. This led to a defeat of Israel at the little
town of Ai, and to a stern warning. God warned Israel,
"Neither will I be with you anymore, unless you
destroy the accursed from among you" (Josh. 7:12).
Achan was identified and executed, and God then continued to aid His people.

God is always present with us. And God is eager to be involved on our behalf. But disobedience can cut us off from His aid. When we deal with our sin and return to Him, the promise of God's involvement in our struggles is ours to claim again.

This particular promise to Joshua was repeated often. Some might say once was enough—and it was. Yet God graciously kept on encouraging Joshua as new situations arose. We also may need to return to God's promises again and again as new situations arise in our lives. God, who kept on encouraging Joshua, will never rebuke us for returning to His promises to claim them over and over again.

—*Larry Richards*

GOD SURROUNDS ME WITH HIS LOVE

"There is no one like the God of Jeshurun, who rides the heavens to help you, and in His excellency on the clouds. The eternal God is your refuge, and underneath are the everlasting arms; He will thrust out the enemy from before you, and will say, 'Destroy!'"

DEUTERONOMY 33:26, 27

These verses show that the Lord is above, around, and underneath His people. We are surrounded by Him, just as the earth is surrounded by the atmosphere:

Within Thy circling power I stand,

On every side I find Thy hand;

Awake, asleep, at home, abroad,

I am surrounded still with God.

The eternal God is our dwelling place and our rest, and underneath are the everlasting arms. A parallel passage is, "His left hand is under my head, and His right hand embraces me" (Song 2:6). The soul has come to its resting place in God and is supported by divine strength. The heart has learned to live in Christ Jesus and to lean on Him day and night.

We are like Noah's dove, weary and about to drop into the destroying waters. But Noah puts out his hand, takes her, and draws her into the ark (Gen. 8:9). She was safe in the hollow of his hand, held with a firm but tender grip. The dove found a refuge that surrounded and upheld her. The hands covered her on all sides.

The hand of God sustains those who dwell in the secret place of the Most High and abide under the shadow of the Almighty. I will say of the Lord, "He is my refuge and my fortress; my God, in Him I will trust" (Ps. 91:1).

—*Charles Haddon Spurgeon*

GOD WILL NOT FORGET ME

"Can a woman forget her nursing child, and not have compassion on the son of her womb? Surely they may forget, yet I will not forget you."

ISAIAH 49:15

"How long, O Lord? Will You forget me forever?" (Ps. 13:1). Can God forget you? Can Omnipotence forget you? Can unchanging love forget you? Can infinite faithfulness forget you? David seemed to think so, and some people who are in deep trouble might agree.

You have been praying for mercy but cannot find it. You think that God forgets. You have been seeking peace but cannot find it. You think that God forgets. Perhaps you were the happiest of the happy as you bathed in the light of God's countenance, but now you are the unhappiest of the unhappy. You are at a distance from God, trying but unable to get back, and you think that God forgets. Wave upon wave of trouble rolls over you. You hardly have time to breathe between the surges of grief, and you are ready to perish with depression. You think God forgets.

That may be how it looks. But it is not possible for God to forget anything. "Can a woman forget her nursing child?" Mark that expression. The child still draws nourishment from her bosom and that is just what you are doing. You think God forgets, but you are living on what He daily gives. You would die if He did not give His grace and strength.

"Can a woman forget her nursing child, and not have compassion on the son of her womb? Surely they may forget, yet I will not forget you" (Is. 49:15). Hold on to this great truth, "I will not forget you."

God has not forgotten to be gracious. God has not forgotten you.

—Charles Haddon Spurgeon

JESUS GUIDES ME WITH HIS LIGHT

"I am the light of the world. He who follows Me shall not walk in darkness, but have the light of life."

JOHN 8:12

In writing his Gospel and his epistles, the apostle John relied frequently on contrasts. Life was contrasted with death. Faith was contrasted with unbelief. Truth was contrasted with falsehood. Light was contrasted with darkness.

The contrast between light and darkness in John is especially significant. Light is necessary to know reality as God sees and knows it. Darkness depicts our human condition, with all our distorted notions about reality and right and wrong. As the light of the world, Jesus is the one who strips away mankind's illusions and reveals righteousness as well as reality.

The apostle John promised in his first epistle that "if we walk in the light as He [God] is in the light, we have fellowship with one another, and the blood of Jesus Christ His Son cleanses us from all sin" (1 John 1:7).

John's image of "walking in darkness" implies great danger. The person who walks in darkness cannot see where he or she is going, and as a result is unable to avoid life's pitfalls. In contrast, a person who has the "light of life"—the life-giving light—can see clearly. He or she can make wise and right decisions that keep one secure.

Proverbs 14:12 declares, "There is a way that seems right to a man, but its end is the way of death." How vital that we rely on God's Word and not our own unaided judgment in choosing what is right in God's eyes. Jesus is the Light of the World. We who follow Him truly have the life-giving light.

—*Larry Richards*

GOD DRAWS ME CLOSE TO HIMSELF

"Draw near to God and He will draw near to you."

JAMES 4:8

This promise flows from a statement James made about God. God is one who "gives grace" (James 4:6). But how are we to receive the grace that God gives? The problem is not with God's willingness to give, but with our readiness to receive grace.

The answer to the question is one of attitude. We are to be humble rather than proud. James went on to spell out in a series of active verbs the characteristics of humble people. The humble:

- submit to God (4:7);
- draw near to God (4:8);
- cleanse their hands (4:8);
- purify their hearts (4:8);
- lament, mourn, and weep (4:9);
- [and thus] humble themselves (4:10).

It is important that we see these as progressive steps. We consciously submit to God. We then draw near to Him, seeking to know and love Him better. Our nearness to God makes us uncomfortable with sin, and we seek to cleanse our hands and to purify our hearts. But in the process we realize how truly sinful we are, and we lament, mourn, and weep. Only then are we truly humbled in God's sight. And then, amazingly, God lifts us up!

When we choose to draw near to God, we can be sure that He will draw near to us. God always responds to believers who want to know Him more intimately. Yet when we claim this promise, we invite God into our lives to do a purifying work which may bring pain before it brings joy. We should take the risk involved in claiming this promise only if we wish to be close to the Lord.

—Larry Richards

GOD IS WATCHING OVER ME

"If I take the wings of the morning, and dwell in the uttermost parts of the sea, even there Your hand shall lead me."

PSALM 139:9, 10

Wherever you are, your heavenly Father watches over you. He looks on you as if there were no other created being in the entire world. His eye is fixed on you every moment.

You cannot banish me from my Lord. Send me to the snows of Siberia, and I will have the eyes of God on me. Send me to the utmost verge of this globe, and I will still have God's eye on me. Put me in the desert, where there is not one blade of grass, and His presence will cheer me.

Let me go to sea in the howling tempest, with winds shrieking, the waves lifting their mad hands to the skies, and I will have the eye of God on me. Let me sink. Let my body lie down in the caverns of the sea, and still the eye of God will be on my very bones.

The eye of God is everywhere. Providence is universal. God's eye is on your friends who are far away.

If you have beloved ones moving, wherever they go, God will keep them.

Wherever you are, whatever your case, God will be with you. His eye is at the wedding, the funeral, the cradle, and the grave. In the battle, God's eye is looking through the smoke. The revolution of God's hand is managing the masses who have broken from their rulers. In the earthquake, the Lord is manifested. In the storm, there is God's hand tossing the ship, dashing it against the rocks, or saving it from the boisterous waves. In all seasons, always, in all dangers, and in all regions of the earth, there is the hand of God.

—*Charles Haddon Spurgeon*

GOD WILL GIVE ME A PLACE IN HEAVEN PREPARED BY JESUS

"And if I go and prepare a place for you, I will come again and receive you to Myself; that where I am, there you may be also."

JOHN 14:3

Chapters 14 through 17 of the Gospel of John contain what is called Christ's "Last Supper Discourse." John welcomes us into the little group that gathered the night before Jesus was crucified to listen to what Jesus taught that fateful night.

This passage has been called the "seedbed of the New Testament," because many important doctrines developed in the New Testament epistles were expressed by Jesus in these chapters in John's Gospel.

The "if I go" in this verse should be read as "since I go." In the Greek language, this is first class conditional, in which the condition is assumed to be fulfilled. Jesus was going to go away to "prepare a place for you" (John 14:2). But His leaving did not mean abandonment. Jesus promised to return. And when Jesus returns, He will take His followers to Himself, to be with Him forever.

In his first letter, John looked ahead to Christ's second coming. He wrote, "Beloved, now we are children of God; and it has not yet been revealed what we shall be, but we know that when He is revealed, we shall be like Him, for we shall see Him as He is" (1 John 3:2). When Jesus returns, He will transform us to make us like Himself.

But this promise has present implications. John adds, "And everyone who has this hope in Him purifies himself, just as He is pure" (1 John 3:3).

How eagerly we should look for Christ to come back. The more we focus on Jesus' return, the greater our motivation will be to live for Jesus now, that we might greet Him with joy rather than shame.

—*Larry Richards*

GOD WILL GIVE ME A GUARANTEED INHERITANCE

"You were sealed with the Holy Spirit of promise, who is the guarantee of our inheritance."

EPHESIANS 1:13, 14

Ephesians 1:3–14 outlines the role of each person of the Trinity in carrying out God's plan of salvation. The Father generated and chose the plan by which believers were to become "holy and without blame before Him in love" (1:4). The Son redeemed us through the blood He shed on Calvary (1:7). And the Holy Spirit enters us, serving as the living guarantee that we will inherit all God has provided for us in Christ.

This passage calls the third person of the Trinity the "Holy Spirit of promise." What commitment is expressed in our possession of the "Holy Spirit of promise"? The Spirit has sealed us. We belong to God, and He will take possession of us when Jesus comes. Because we trust in Jesus our salvation is assured.

God expects us to *know* our eternal destiny. Verses such as John 3:36 speak with a certain voice: "He who believes in the Son has everlasting life; and he who does not believe in the Son shall not see life, but the wrath of God abides on him." There is no "I hope" and no "maybe" in John 3:36. And there is no uncertainty about our sealing by the Holy Spirit of promise, who is Himself God's guarantee of heaven.

Our certainty is based on the realization that salvation is a gift, purchased on Calvary. We will be in heaven because of what Christ has done for us—not because of anything we have done. Rather than feeling more holy than others, we who know we will be in heaven are more aware of being sinners who have no hope in ourselves. All the credit and glory for our salvation belongs to Jesus.

—*Larry Richards*

GOD WILL GIVE ME HEAVENLY TREASURES RATHER THAN EARTHLY RICHES

"Jesus said to him, 'If you want to be perfect, go, sell what you have and give to the poor, and you will have treasure in heaven; and come, follow Me.'"

MATTHEW 19:21

A wealthy young man came to Jesus, asking what he had to do to gain eternal life. Jesus' demand that he sell all called for a greater sacrifice than we can imagine. In the Mediterranean world, to "sell all" would mean the sale of the family home and land. And to top it off, Jesus required that he reject his family in favor of a relationship with Jesus and a surrogate family formed by Jesus' followers!

The wealthy young man turned away regretfully, unwilling to make this kind of sacrifice, even for a place and treasure in the world to come.

The young man's response revealed that his heart was far from God. In a choice between wealth and Jesus, money won. And in choosing his wealth, the young man broke the first and greatest of the commandments—to have no other God than the one supreme Lord.

The incident was an effort by Jesus to reveal to the young man his lostness. It was also a warning to us that nothing must be allowed to take Christ's place in our hearts.

Later, Jesus was asked by His disciples what they would gain. After all, they had turned their back on all they held dear to follow Christ. Jesus replied there was a special place reserved in eternity for the Twelve (Matt. 19:28). And for all who follow Jesus, there is not only treasure in heaven, but also greater rewards in this life than we would have experienced had we chosen not to become His followers (Matt. 19:29).

—*Larry Richards*

GOD ACCEPTS ME AS ONE OF HIS CHILDREN

"But love your enemies, do good, and lend, hoping for nothing in return; and your reward will be great, and you will be sons of the Most High."

LUKE 6:35

Luke 6 contains Jesus' "sermon on the plain" (cf. Luke 6:17). It contains much of the same material included in His more famous Sermon on the Mount (Matt. 5–7). Christ must have often repeated the themes found in these two sermons, which emphasized the way of life to be adopted by those who follow Him.

Jesus promised those who imitate God in the way they deal with enemies that they would be given a great reward. The promise is conditional; the reward is for those who love their enemies, do good, and who "lend, hoping for nothing in return." This last phrase refers to some benefit in addition to repayment of the principal. Jesus was saying that a person should help the helpless as well as make interest-free loans to friends who can later do favors in return.

But rewards are not the reason we should love enemies. The reason believers should act in this way is

that it is appropriate for children to resemble their
fathers. Jesus does not imply that a person can earn
sonship (cf. John 1:12, 13). He simply says that God's
children ought to pattern their lives on the example set
by their heavenly Father.

It is one thing to recognize a moral obligation and
quite another to fulfill it. What sets Jesus' teaching
apart is the realization that only those who become
sons of God through faith in Christ can become like
the Father. Christ is not telling sinners to try to be like
God. He is reminding sons of God to be who they are!

The promise of reward is ours to claim today. We
do so by relating to others as God in mercy and love
relates to us.

—*Larry Richards*

GOD WILL SHOW ME THE FULL REVELATION OF JESUS IN THE FUTURE

"Jesus answered and said to him, 'Because I said to you, "I saw you under the fig tree," do you believe? . . . Most assuredly, I say to you, hereafter you shall see heaven open, and the angels of God ascending and descending upon the Son of Man.'"

JOHN 1:50, 51

After spending a day with Jesus, Philip hurried to tell his brother Nathanael that he had discovered the Messiah. As the two approached, Jesus commented on Nathanael's spotless character. The surprised Nathanael asked how Jesus knew him. Jesus replied, "Before Philip called you, when you were under the fig tree, I saw you."

Nathanael immediately grasped the implications of Christ's supernatural knowledge, and said, "You are the Son of God! You are the king of Israel!" (John 1:49). In response to this confession of faith, Jesus promised that Nathanael would see greater things than these—

that is, greater than the knowledge He had displayed of Nathanael.

Jesus promised future supernatural revelation. Nathanael would see heaven open and the angels ascending and descending upon Jesus as the Son of Man. Jesus' promise was that one day in the future, Nathanael would see Jesus come from heaven with His mighty angels. Then Christ will appear as Son of Man, a title drawn from Daniel 7:13, 14. This mysterious figure will be invested by God with universal authority.

What Jesus was saying is that the one whom Nathanael recognized by faith would one day be revealed to all, and that Nathanael would witness that great day. The promise given to Nathanael is ours as well. Today we recognize Jesus as the Son of God. Tomorrow, when Jesus returns, we will witness and share in His final triumph.

—*Larry Richards*

GOD PROMISES THAT I WILL APPEAR WITH JESUS IN GLORY

"When Christ who is our life appears, then you also will appear with Him in glory."

COLOSSIANS 3:4

We live in a material universe that consists of things. John described the materialist, who sought the meaning of life in this universe, as "loving" the world. But John warned that "all that is in the world—the lust of the flesh, the lust of the eyes, and the pride of life—is not of the Father but is of the world" (1 John 2:16).

Here in Colossians Paul reminded Christians that we have been raised with Christ. Thus we are to "set [our] minds on things above, not on things on the earth" (Col. 3:2). A passion for wealth, honor, power, or pleasures is not appropriate behavior for those who have been raised in Christ to a higher level.

The wellspring and source of our new life "is hidden with Christ in God" (Col. 3:3). What motivates us cannot be seen or understood by people of the world. One day Jesus will return to earth. His return is called an appearance, because then He will be visible to all. When Jesus returns, "you also will appear with Him in glory."

Today the world may ridicule Christian values or condemn Christian commitment to what God says is just and right. But the realities that guide us are hidden from the people of the world. Paul tells us that when Jesus returns and is revealed to all, we will appear with Him in glory. Our true identity and splendor as children of God will be displayed to everyone when we appear with Jesus in glory.

When Jesus comes, we will appear with Him in glory. Our choice of Christ and His ways will be vindicated. And those who ridiculed "will give an account to Him who is ready to judge the living and the dead" (1 Pet. 4:5).

—*Larry Richards*

GOD WILL REWARD MY LABORS OF LOVE FOR OTHERS

"For God is not unjust to forget your work and labor of love which you have shown toward His name, in that you have ministered to the saints, and do minister."

HEBREWS 6:10

The writer of Hebrews had just urged his readers to go on in their Christian lives and not to return to foundational salvation truths. The believer who is sure of his or her salvation is free to focus on producing fruit. Those who doubt their salvation become unproductive.

The writer of Hebrews let his readers know that he did not consider them unproductive. In fact, he was "confident of better things concerning you, yes, things that accompany salvation" (Heb. 6:9). In the following promise verse, the writer pointed to evidence that his readers' Christian lives had been productive, and assured them that God would not "forget" their service.

"Forget" and "remember" are not primarily mental terms in the Bible, especially when ascribed to God.

They are action words. To remember means *to act on what is remembered*. Thus, when God's Old Testament people turned back to Him after sinning, the Scripture often notes that "God remembered His covenant" and came to their aid or helped them (cf. Lev. 26:42, 45).

To remember the covenant means that God acted to keep the covenant promises He had made to Israel. In the same way, for God to forget or fail to remember our sins (cf. Ps. 25:7; Is. 43:25) means that God will not punish us as our sins deserve. He chooses instead to forgive us. Here, then, Scripture's word that God will not "forget your work and labor of love" is a promise of reward.

This promise is rooted in God's nature as a "rewarder of those who diligently seek Him" (Heb. 11:6). God will reward us graciously when we commit ourselves to labors of love in ministering to His saints.

—*Larry Richards*

GOD WILL GIVE ME ETERNAL LIFE

"Be faithful until death, and I will give you the crown of life."

REVELATION 2:10

Carlyle, in his *History of the French Revolution*, tells of the Duke of Orleans who did not believe in death. One day his secretary stumbled on the words, "The late king of Spain," and the duke angrily demanded what he meant by that remark. The secretary responded, "My Lord, it is a title that some of the kings have taken."

We are immortal. God has endowed us with a spiritual nature that will outlive the sun, outlast the stars, and exist throughout eternity. When the righteous soul leaves the body, it appears before God. "Assuredly, I say to you, today you will be with Me in Paradise" (Luke 23:43).

Christ, however, has not only bought His people's souls, but also their bodies. Our bodies will be raised, and our souls will re-enter our bodies. Here we are a shriveled grain, sown in the earth, but our next body will have all the loveliness that heaven can give. It will be a glorious body, raised in honor, raised in power, raised to die no more (1 Cor. 16:54).

Let me wave the palm of victory (Rev. 7:9). Let me wear the crown of life (Rev. 2:10). Let me wear the fine white linen of immaculate perfection (Rev. 19:8). Let me cast my crown before Jehovah's throne (Rev. 4:10). Let me sing the everlasting song. Let my voice join the eternal chorus, "Alleluia! For the Lord God Omnipotent reigns!" (Rev. 19:6). My voice will be sweetly tuned to the notes of gratitude, and my heart will dance with ecstasy before the throne.

"He who testifies to these things says, 'Surely I am coming quickly.' Amen. Even so, come, Lord Jesus" (Rev. 22:20).

—Charles Haddon Spurgeon

GOD WILL GIVE ME A CROWN OF RIGHTEOUSNESS

"Finally, there is laid up for me the crown of right-eousness, which the Lord, the righteous Judge, will give to me on that Day."

2 TIMOTHY 4:8

The "crown" in this verse is not a royal crown (a *diadema*) but the crown made of leaves (*stephanos*) awarded to the victor in an athletic contest. While the victor's crown of leaves had no monetary value, it was greatly prized. It represented an achievement that brought honor to the athlete and to the city he represented.

When the apostle Paul looked back at his life as a race run for the Lord, he expressed confidence that Christ Himself would award Paul the victor's crown. This type of crown is available to every believer who loves Christ's appearing.

The crown is described as a "crown of righteous-ness." The phrase is somewhat ambiguous in Greek. It may mean "the crown appropriate for the righteous man," or "the crown won by righteousness," or even

"the crown that consists of (eternal) righteousness."
We can settle on the second of these possibilities when
we see the implications of his promise that this same
crown will be awarded "all those who have loved His
appearing."

There are three Greek words used in speaking of
Jesus' return. *Parousia* emphasizes Jesus' coming to be
with us. *Apocolypsis* emphasizes Jesus' coming as the
ultimate unveiling of reality. The word used here,
epiphaneia, "emphasizes the fact that Jesus' return will
constitute a disrupting intervention in a world that
remains blind to God's grace. Shattered by His appearing, the world system of today will be replaced by the
long-awaited kingdom of righteousness, and evil will
be judged" (*Expository Dictionary of Bible Words,* 1985,
p. 66).

Thus, to love Jesus' appearing as *epiphaneia* is to be
fully dedicated to Him. We should love nothing in this
world so much that it draws us away from our commitment to Christ and God's will.

—*Larry Richards*

God Will Give Me a Glorious Spiritual Body

"For we know that if our earthly house, this tent, is destroyed, we have a building from God, a house not made with hands, eternal in the heavens."

—2 Corinthians 5:1

This poor body of ours, which at times is so full of aches and pains, will one day be taken away to make room for a more glorious one. This one is getting worn out; some parts of it have already fallen away. It is like a very old building, which cannot last much longer and seldom stands to the end of the ninety-nine year lease. It soon crumbles and, by-and-by with all of us, the old house will fall to pieces and be done with.

Shall we then worry? Shall our soul cry concerning the body, "Alas my sister! Alas my brother"? No! "He takes away the first that He may establish the second" (Heb. 10:9). As we have carried the image of the earthly in this body of humiliation, we will, in the second condition of this body, carry the image of the heavenly. "The body is sown in corruption, it is raised in incorruption. It is sown in dishonor, it is raised in glory. It is sown in weakness, it is raised in power. It is sown a natural body, it is raised a spiritual body" (1 Cor. 15:42–44).

"He takes away the first that He may establish the second." And what a glorious second that will be! Our resurrection body will know no pain, no weariness, no weakness, no sign of disease, no sin, and no possibility of corruption or death.

Well may we sing: "O glorious hour! O blessed abode!"

Since this poor body will be made like the glorious body of Christ Jesus our Savior, let the first body go, without a murmur or a sigh.

—Charles Haddon Spurgeon

TOPICAL INDEX

God's Promises Related to:

ACCESS TO GOD, 32, 36, 92, 168
See also *Fellowship with God.*

ADDICTIONS, 132

AFFLICTION, 20, 54, 70, 122, 126, 208
See also *Trials; Troubles.*

ANXIETY, 18, 26, 140, 194
See also *Worry.*

ASSURANCE, 48, 62, 150, 190, 210, 224, 242, 244
See also *Comfort.*

BELIEF, 56
See also *Faith; Trust.*

BEREAVEMENT, 196, 216
See also *Death; Grief; Loss.*

BLESSING, 10, 12, 14, 16, 18, 20, 22, 24, 26, 28, 30, 32, 34, 36, 38, 40, 42, 44, 46, 72, 230

BREAD OF LIFE, 184

BURDENS, 18, 24, 34, 70, 84, 112

CERTAINTY, 104
See also *Doubt; Faith; Uncertainty.*

CHILDREN, 58
See also *Loved Ones.*

CHRIST THE MEDIATOR, 34

CHRISTIAN LIVING, 102, 104, 162, 180, 186
See also *Discipline; Spiritual Growth.*

COMFORT, 26, 66, 68, 150, 210
See also *Assurance.*

CONFLICT, 98
See also *Oneness in Christ.*

CONFUSION, 238
See also *Frustration; Uncertainty.*

CONTENTMENT, 28, 116
See also *Peace.*

DEATH, 62, 66, 68, 124, 196, 198, 212, 216
See also *Bereavement; Loss; Grief.*

DECISIONS, 96
See also *Discernment; Will of God.*

DELIVERANCE, 54, 72, 76, 78, 82, 88, 120, 198

DEPRESSION, 18, 72, 118, 134, 136, 198, 244

DESPAIR, 20, 54, 124, 134, 135
See also *Hope.*

DISAPPOINTMENT, 70

DISCERNMENT, 94, 96, 100, 246
See also *Decisions; Will of God.*

DISCIPLINE, 122, 126, 128
See also *Patience; Persecution.*

DISCOURAGEMENT, 90, 124, 136
See also *Encouragement.*

DISOBEDIENCE, 132
See also *Obedience to God.*

DIVORCE, 58

DOUBT, 18, 94, 138
See also *Faith; Certainty; Uncertainty.*

ENCOURAGEMENT, 232, 240, 250
See also *Discouragement.*

ETERNAL LIFE, 46, 56, 182, 184, 266

FAILURE, 232
See also *Success.*

FAITH, 40, 42, 46, 56, 94, 106, 110, 126, 134, 138, 164, 166, 172, 174, 176, 180, 184, 198, 228, 258
See also *Belief; Certainty; Trust.*

FAITHFULNESS OF GOD, 76, 82, 114, 192, 204, 214, 244

FEAR, 50, 60, 62, 66, 110, 212, 250

FELLOWSHIP WITH GOD, 148, 154, 156, 160, 186, 218, 248, 258
See also *Access to God.*

FORGIVENESS, 12, 46, 130, 156, 164, 170, 172, 204
See also *Love of God.*

FREEDOM IN CHRIST, 28, 38, 78

FRUITFULNESS, 38, 200, 226, 264
See also *Serving God; Usefulness.*

FRUSTRATION, 80, 84
See also *Confusion; Uncertainty.*

GLORY, 160, 210, 228, 260, 262

GOSPEL OF GRACE, 30, 152

GRACE OF GOD, 12, 24, 30, 52, 118, 128, 130, 138, 174, 176, 228
See also *Love of God.*

GRIEF, 196, 216
See also *Bereavement; Death; Loss.*

GUIDANCE OF GOD, 48, 90, 92, 94, 96, 100, 104, 108, 246

HEALING, 130, 132, 136, 142, 144, 202
See also *Pain; Sickness; Suffering.*

HEAVEN, 68, 234, 252, 254, 256, 262, 266, 270
See also *Treasure in Heaven.*

HOLINESS, 102, 156, 186, 248

HOLY SPIRIT, 10, 26, 32, 36, 38, 80, 84, 86, 92, 96, 106, 108, 150, 162, 180, 220, 254

HOPE, 110, 138, 154, 210
See also *Despair.*

HUNGER, 44
See also *Material Needs; Poverty.*

INHERITANCE, 90, 254
See also *Rewards.*

JOY IN THE LORD, 16, 198, 210, 228, 262

LEADERSHIP, 84

LIGHT OF THE WORLD, 246

LIVING WATER, 182

LONELINESS, 122

LOSS, 122, 142, 196
See also *Bereavement; Death; Grief.*

LOVED ONES, 58, 124, 196, 216
See also *Children.*

LOVE OF GOD, 12, 20, 50, 58, 128, 150, 164, 166, 170, 172, 174, 178, 180, 192, 198, 202, 204, 206, 242, 244
See also *Grace of God.*

MATERIAL NEEDS, 44, 116, 124, 142, 194
See also *Hunger; Poverty.*

MEANING AND PURPOSE, 16, 154, 158, 160, 162
See also *Self-Worth; Significance.*

MERCY, 24, 52, 64, 138

MESSIAH, 92

MIND OF CHRIST, 106

OBEDIENCE TO GOD, 16, 22, 74, 78, 82, 132, 146, 188, 200, 218, 226, 240, 248, 256, 268
See also *Disobedience.*

OLD AGE, 64, 124

ONENESS IN CHRIST, 30, 32, 98
See also *Conflict.*

PAIN, 118, 124, 136, 198
See also *Healing; Sickness; Suffering.*

PATIENCE, 118
See also *Discipline; Persecution.*

PEACE, 22, 26, 62, 86, 102, 140
See also *Contentment.*

PERSECUTION, 118, 206
See also *Discipline; Patience.*

POVERTY, 124
See also *Hunger; Material Needs.*

POWER, 40, 74, 80, 142, 146, 174, 222, 226
See also *Strength from God; Weakness.*

PRAYER, 10, 32, 40, 70, 144, 200

PRESENCE OF GOD, 20, 36, 38, 48, 64, 112, 120, 150, 158, 192, 202, 204, 208, 222, 224, 236, 238, 240, 242, 244, 246, 248, 250

PROTECTION, 26, 42, 48, 50, 58, 60, 64, 82, 88, 120, 158, 168, 202, 206, 236, 242, 244, 250

PROVISION, 42, 52, 90, 116, 168, 182, 184, 194

REST, 22, 24, 104

RESTORATION, 130, 138, 142, 164, 186

RESURRECTION, 68, 152, 196, 212, 216, 234, 252, 262, 266, 270

REWARDS, 50, 66, 68, 104, 152, 178, 210, 212, 216, 234, 252, 254, 256, 258, 260, 262, 264, 266, 268, 270

RIGHTEOUSNESS, 80, 102, 156, 162, 166, 174, 176, 178, 204, 268

ROLE MODELS, 102

SADNESS, 124, 134

SALVATION, 30, 46, 56, 152, 164, 166, 168, 170, 172, 174, 176, 178, 180, 186, 188, 190, 204, 214, 254
See also *Transformation.*

SECOND COMING OF CHRIST, 210, 214, 216, 252, 254, 260, 262, 266, 268

SECURITY, 60, 62, 204, 206, 242

SELF-PITY, 72

SELF-WORTH, 148, 154, 158, 160, 162, 188, 218, 220, 222, 232
See also *Meaning and Purpose; Significance.*

SERVING GOD, 112, 218, 220, 222, 224, 226, 228, 230, 232, 234, 264

SICKNESS, 122, 124, 144, 202
See also *Healing; Pain; Suffering.*

SIGNIFICANCE, 148, 154, 158, 160, 162, 188, 218, 220, 222, 232
See also *Meaning and Purpose; Self-Worth.*

SORROW, 20, 124, 208
See also *Bereavement; Grief.*

SPIRITUAL GIFTS, 10, 220

SPIRITUAL GROWTH, 42, 102, 114, 122, 126, 128, 162, 170, 180, 184, 190, 220, 226, 238, 258, 264
See also *Christian Living; Discipline.*

SPIRITUAL WARFARE, 74
See also *Temptation.*

STRENGTH FROM GOD, 20, 52, 88, 112, 114, 126, 128, 132, 134, 144, 146, 222, 224, 228, 236, 242, 248
See also *Power; Weakness.*

SUCCESS, 224
See also *Failure.*

SUFFERING, 128, 198, 230
See also *Healing; Pain; Sickness.*

SUPPLY, 52, 116, 168, 182, 184, 194

TEMPTATION, 60, 74, 76, 114
See also *Spiritual Warfare.*

TRANSFORMATION, 80, 160, 162, 180, 188, 190, 216, 252
See also *Salvation.*

TREASURE IN HEAVEN, 116, 256
See also *Heaven.*

TRIALS, 54, 72, 76, 86, 110, 118, 126, 140, 208, 230
See also *Affliction; Troubles.*

TROUBLES, 34, 54, 70, 86, 140, 208, 238, 240, 244
See also *Affliction; Trials.*

TRUST, 34, 40, 44, 46, 64, 94, 104, 172, 176, 180
See also *Belief; Certainty; Faith.*

TRUTH, 100, 108, 156

UNCERTAINTY, 208, 212
See also *Certainty; Doubt; Faith; Frustration.*

UNDERSTANDING, 14
See also *Wisdom.*

USEFULNESS, 232
See also *Fruitfulness.*

VICTORY, 74, 76, 86, 120, 198

WEAKNESS, 64, 134, 146, 228
See also *Power; Strength from God.*

WILL OF GOD, 22, 40, 92, 94, 96, 100, 106, 118, 200, 246
See also *Discernment; Obedience to God.*

WISDOM, 14, 94, 108
See also *Understanding.*

WORRY, 194
See also *Anxiety.*

SCRIPTURE INDEX

Page numbers where Scripture passages appear are printed in bold italic type.

GENESIS
1:1, *154*; 1:26, *149*; 1:27, *148*; 3:21, *174*; 3:22, *186*; 3:24, *186*; 8:9, *243*; 12:1–3,7, *176*; 15:1, *50*; 15:6, *176*; 21:13, *58*; 22:15–18, *177*; 24:7, *106*; 24:40, *106*; 28:15, *236*

EXODUS
3:1, *232*; 3:12, *222*; 3:18, *224*; 3:20, *224*; 14:13, *18*; 14:14, *238*; 16:4, *42*; 18:13–23, *84*; 23:20, *82*; 32:34, *82*; 33:2, *82*

LEVITICUS
4:2,13,22,27, *172*; 4:35, *172*; 5:15, *172*; 16:30, *172*; 26:42,45, *265*

NUMBERS
11:17, *84*; 11:24–25, *84*

DEUTERONOMY
6:4, *24*; 8:3, *42*; 13:1–5, *93*; 18:15, *92*; 18:18, *92*; 31:6,8, *222*; 33:25, *76, 113*; 33:26–27, *242*

JOSHUA
1:5, *222, 240*; 1:5,9, *238*; 1:9, *240*; 7:12, *240*; 10:18, *240*; 11:16, *240*; 23:10, *240*

JUDGES
2:1, *83*

1 SAMUEL
3:10, *96*

2 SAMUEL
11:1–17, *132–133*; 12:20, *21*; 21:9, *97*; 22:37, *111*

1 KINGS
3:12-13, *14*; 4:16, *131*; 4:29–34, *14*; 8:27, *130*; 8:56, *8*;
18:22, *72*; 18:40, *72*; 19:4, *72, 134*; 19:13, *72*; 21:27,29, *12*

2 KINGS
6:6, *110*

1 CHRONICLES
4:10, *116–117*; 28:20, *222*

2 CHRONICLES
7:14, *130*; 20:17, *88*

JOB
2:10, *124*; 5:19, *35*; 9:5–6, *62*; 16:2, *137*; 39:13–15, *202*;
42:10, *142*

PSALMS
13:1, *244*; 22:11, *209*; 23:1, *90*; 23:4, *68, 212*; 25:7, *265*;
25:18, *198*; 27:9, *209*; 32:8, *206*; 34:18, *136–137*; 37:3–4,
35, 45; 38:21, *208*; 50:15, *34, 70–71*; 59:16, *206*;
84:11–12, *35*; 88:18, *137*; 89:33–34, *193*; 91:1, *243*; 91:4,
209; 94:14, *34*; 94:19, *18–19*; 100:3, *203*; 116:15, *197*;
119:117, *208*; 119:67, *126*; 126:2–3, *73*; 136:1, *64, 150*;
139:9–10, *250*

PROVERBS
14:12, *247*; 27:1, *210–211*

SONG OF SOLOMON
2:6, *242*; 2:11, *212*; 2:12, *212–213*; 2:13, *213*; 5:1, *140*

ISAIAH
1:15–20, *164*; 1:18, *164*; 11:11, *30*; 40:30–31, *146*; 43:1, *54*; 43:2, *21*, *54*; 43:25, *193*, *265*; 46:4, *64*; 48:10, *122*; 49:15, *244–245*; 49:16, *206*; 55:11, *225*; 57:20–21, *23*

JEREMIAH
3:22, *132*; 6:16, *22*; 16:19, *30*; 31:3, *150–151*; 33:3, *138*; 33:6, *138*

LAMENTATIONS
3:21–23, *151*; 3:23, *192*; 3:32, *20–21*

EZEKIEL
34:23, *168*

DANIEL
7:13–14, *261*

MALACHI
3:17, *48–49*

MATTHEW
3:7, *167*; 4:4, *43*; 6:11, *45*; 6:12, *171*; 6:14–15, *170*; 6:26, *34*, *194*; 6:31–34, *194*; 6:32, *195*; 6:33, *15*; 7:11, *10*; 10:39, *188*; 11:28, *24*; 12:1–8, *25*; 14:13–21, *44*; 15:32–38, *44*; 16:18, *63*; 16:25–26, *188*; 17:20, *40*; 18:15, *98*; 18:16, *98*; 18:17, *98*; 18:18, *98*; 19:21, *256*; 19:28, *257*; 19:29, *257*; 21:21–22, *40*; 24:24, *206*; 24:44, *210*

MARK
1:17, *218*; 1:18, *218*; 15:34, *230*

LUKE
6:17, *258*; 6:35, *258*; 11:4, *75*; 11:9, *10*; 11:9–13, *10*; 11:13,

150; 12:7, *158*; 12:25, *194*; 12:32, *62*; 18:27, *110*; 21:8, *158*; 21:17–18, *158*; 21:17–19, *158*; 23:43, *266*

JOHN
1:12-13, *259*; 1:49, *260*; 1:50–51, *260*; 3:16, *46, 56*; 3:36, *56, 167, 255*; 4:14, *182*; 6:51, *184*; 7:17, *100, 156*; 8:12, *246*; 8:13–29; *78*; 8:31–32, *78, 108*; 8:33–59, *78*; 10:9, *168*; 10:14, *203*; 10:27–28, *76*; 10:28, *206*; 10:29, *54, 206*; 11:35, *197*; 12:23–27, *152*; 12:32, *152*; 12:33, *152*; 14:2, *253*; 14:3, *252*; 14:16–17, *36*; 15:4, *17*; 15:5, *226*; 15:7, *200*; 15:10, *227*; 15:12, *227*; 15:16, *227*; 16:13, *108*; 16:33, *86*; 17:15, *61*; 17:18, *61*; 17:24, *196*; 21:5, *44*; 21:9, *45*; 21:12, *44*

ACTS
5:1, *170*

ROMANS
1:16–3:23, *166*; 1:18, *167*; 3:24, *166*; 4:4–5, *176*; 4:7, *170*; 5:6–8, *204*; 5:9, *166*; 5:10, *160*; 5:11, *166*; 5:12, *174*; 8:1, *213*; 8:9, *37*; 8:10, *205*; 8:11, *80*; 8:28, *162*; 8:29, *163*; 8:31, *112, 204*; 8:33, *204*; 8:38–39, *204, 207*; 9:22, *167*

1 CORINTHIANS
1:4–8, *178*; 1:7, *178*; 1:8, *178*; 2:16, *93, 107*; 4:5, *235*; 5:1–5, *99*; 10:13, *76–77, 114*; 12:1, *220*; 12:7, *37, 220*; 13:4–8, *119*; 15:42–44, *271*; 15:51, *217*; 15:58, *225, 234–235*

2 CORINTHIANS
2:5–8, *99*; 5:1, *270*; 5:8, *68–69*; 5:10, *234*; 5:14, *179*; 5:15–16, *178*; 5:17, *180–181*; 12:7, *228*; 12:9, *228*

GALATIANS
5:16, *38*; 5:19–21, *38*; 5:22–23, *38*

EPHESIANS
1:4, *151, 254*; 1:7, *170, 254*; 1:13–14, *254*; 2:3, *167*; 2:4–5, *53*; 2:10, *54*; 2:16, *33*; 2:18, *32*; 3:6; *30*; 3:10, *31*

PHILIPPIANS
1:6, *190–191*; 1:23, *212*; 2:12, *191*; 2:13, *191*; 4:6–7, *26*; 4:8, *102*; 4:9, *102*; 4:19, *28*

COLOSSIANS
2:15, *74*; 3:2, *262*; 3:3, *262*; 3:4, *262*

1 THESSALONIANS
4:12, *111*; 4:13, *197*; 4:13–18, *216*; 4:16, *68*; 4:16–17, *216*; 4:17, *63*

2 THESSALONIANS
1:6–10, *167*; 3:3, *60*; 3:16, *140–141*

1 TIMOTHY
2:5, *34*

2 TIMOTHY
4:8, *268*

HEBREWS
4:1,9, *104*; 4:11, *105*; 4:12, *104*; 4:13, *104*; 4:15, *140*; 4:16, *52*; 6:9, *264*; 6:10, *264*; 9:28, *214*; 10:9, *270*; 10:10–12,14, *173*; 11:6, *265*; 12:11, *128*; 12:12, *128*; 12:12–17, *128*; 12:13, *129*; 12:15, *129*; 13:5, *112*; 13:6, *120–121*; 13:20, *48*

JAMES
1:2, *118*; 1:2–3, *126*; 1:5, *15, 94*; 1:6–8, *94*; 1:12, *114, 210*; 1:13–17, *114*; 1:17, *150*; 4:3, *11*; 4:6, *248*; 4:7, *74, 248*; 4:8, *248*; 4:9, *248*; 4:10, *248*; 5:15, *144*

1 PETER
1:18–19, *54*; 4:5, *263*; 5:4, *48*

2 PETER
1:8, *16*

1 JOHN
1:7, *156, 246*; 1:8, *157*; 1:9, *13*; 2:16, *262*; 3:2, *160, 253*; 3:3, *253*

REVELATION
1:17, *66*; 2:10, *266–267*; 4:10, *267*; 5:13, *211*; 7:9, *211, 267*; 17:8, *54*; 19:6, *267*; 19:8, *267*; 21:4, *211*; 21:18, *211*; 22:20, *267*